The Department Chair:
New Roles, Responsibilities and Challenges

by Alan T. Seagren, John W. Creswell, and Daniel W. Wheeler

ASHE-ERIC Higher Education Report No. 1, 1993

Prepared by

Clearinghouse on Higher Education
The George Washington University

In cooperation with

Association for the Study
of Higher Education

Published by

School of Education and Human Development
The George Washington University

Jonathan D. Fife, Series Editor

Cite as

Seagren, Alan T., John W. Creswell, and Daniel W. Wheeler. 1993. *The Department Chair: New Roles, Responsibilities and Challenges.* ASHE-ERIC Higher Education Report No. 1. Washington, D.C.: The George Washington University, School of Education and Human Development.

Library of Congress Catalog Card Number 93-86309
ISSN 0884-0040
ISBN 1-878380-22-2

Managing Editor: Bryan Hollister
Manuscript Editor: Barbara Fishel, Editech
Cover design by Michael David Brown, Rockville, Maryland

The ERIC Clearinghouse on Higher Education invites individuals to submit proposals for writing monographs for the *ASHE-ERIC Higher Education Report* series. Proposals must include:
1. A detailed manuscript proposal of not more than five pages.
2. A chapter-by-chapter outline.
3. A 75-word summary to be used by several review committees for the initial screening and rating of each proposal.
4. A vita and a writing sample.

ERIC Clearinghouse on Higher Education
School of Education and Human Development
The George Washington University
One Dupont Circle, Suite 630
Washington, DC 20036-1183

This publication was prepared partially with funding from the Office of Educational Research and Improvement, U.S. Department of Education, under contract no. ED RI-88-062014. The opinions expressed in this report do not necessarily reflect the positions or policies of OERI or the Department.

EXECUTIVE SUMMARY

The academic department is the base unit of universities and colleges, "the central building block . . . of the American university" (Trow 1977). While departments fragment and divide the faculty of an institution of higher education, they also provide a useful structure for the day-to-day activities that shape faculty members' attitudes, behaviors, and performances.

The metaphor of a block of wood held in a vise for shaping seems appropriate to describe the situation of an academic chair. The chair is squeezed between the demands of upper administration and institutional expectations on the one side and the expectations of faculty, staff, and students on the other, with both attempting to influence and shape the chair. The chair is caught in the middle, required to provide the most sophisticated leadership and statesmanship to avoid being crushed by these two opposing forces.

The purpose of *The Department Chair* is to glean from the research insights about the chairs or heads of academic departments who are caught in the middle. The literature documents that chairs of academic departments in the 1990s will be expected to perform in an increasingly complex, diverse, and changing environment, with ever-increasing expectations from the institution and the faculty. The following issues, discussed in *The Department Chair,* are most often raised as needing attention: (1) roles and responsibilities of chairs, (2) the chair as leader, (3) the political influences on the chair and the use of power, (4) the chair's responsibility for evaluation and development of faculty, (5) the influence of institutional type and specific discipline on the chair, and (6) challenges facing chairs in the 1990s and beyond.

What Are the Roles and Responsibilities of Chairs?

Numerous studies have been conducted on the tasks, activities, roles, and responsibilities of departmental chairs, but despite researchers' ability to identify tasks and job-related duties, the chair's role continues to be ambiguous, unclear in terms of authority, and unable to be classified as faculty or administrator—all of which contribute to a high level of stress. Thus, the chair must learn to cope readily with the demands of being in the middle, with responsibilities to both faculty and administration.

What Are the Requirements for Leadership?

Institutions of higher education differ from many organizations, requiring leadership to be a more shared phenomenon than in most profit-focused enterprises. The concept of faculty ownership is basic to academic institutions; thus, departmental leadership requires greater emphasis on empowering activities than in many other types of organizations. The chair, in concert with faculty, must develop a vision beyond the immediate tasks and employ strategies that develop the faculty's commitment to that vision. While chairs have opportunities to exercise leadership in a number of different settings, including faculty meetings, offices and laboratories, the total institution, and the disciplinary community, the requirements of leadership vary depending on the department's stage of development, the specific management function, the academic discipline, and the chair's own style of leadership. The chair must ensure that an effective data base exists for informed decision making, try to understand the use and dynamics of the politics of the institution, use faculty members' strengths to develop quality, and create an environment where faculty can strengthen their own professional status through the achievement of a shared vision.

How Can the Chair Effectively Use Political Influence and Power?

A number of internal and external constituencies—faculty, upper-level administration, the institution's governing body, legislative bodies, accrediting bodies, other external agencies and groups—influence decision making in the department. Institutions of higher education are, to a large extent, open political systems. Chairs draw upon two primary sources of power: the authority outlined in formal job descriptions and the informal influence of personal characteristics, expertise, and ability to capitalize on opportunity. Chairs must understand the political forces and processes of the institution and must skillfully maneuver groups and coalitions to achieve the autonomy and control necessary to develop a strong department. Chairs must skillfully use certain strategies (called push, pull, persuasion, preventative, and preparatory strategies in the literature) and tactics (impression management, agenda setting, networking, and negotiation) to manage an effective department.

What Is the Chair's Role in Faculty Evaluation and Development?

The quality of the program of an academic department is largely determined by the quality and performance of the faculty. Evaluation, the process of making judgments about performance, is one of the most powerful opportunities for developing quality available to a chair.

For a chair to evaluate faculty effectively, the reasons for the evaluation and the techniques to be employed must be clear to the chair, the dean, and the faculty. Procedures to evaluate faculty can provide focus, clarify expectations for work, give direction to faculty members' efforts, and define the need for faculty development. What is to be measured, how it is to be measured, who is to measure, and the indicators of quality must be carefully considered. The chair must provide that leadership in developing and implementing evaluation of the faculty (Braskamp, Brandenburg, and Ory 1984).

A second and equally powerful opportunity to encourage quality is faculty development—the process of assisting faculty to grow professionally by gaining an understanding of institutional expectations, improving performance in teaching or research, creating a positive work environment, refocusing or redirecting activities, and helping faculty resolve and deal with personal issues. Faculty development is a shared responsibility that can be facilitated through a number of activities and strategies, including orientation sessions, mentoring, intervention in teaching and research, providing models of desired behaviors, considering alternative professional career paths, and assisting faculty in using available resources, such as employee assistance programs.

What Are the Influences of Institutional Type and Discipline on the Chair?

The roles and responsibilities of and expectations for the chair are all influenced by the type of institution and by differences in methodology and body of knowledge of specific academic disciplines. The chair must recognize how institutional type, history, and culture, model of governance, and discipline can influence what is expected of him or her, in turn determining the most effective strategies to use. Chairs should take advantage of opportunities for professional development through programs offered by a number of organizations, institutions, and professional associations.

What Does the Future Hold?

Institutions of higher education face a number of challenges in the remainder of the 1990s and beyond: quality, diversity and gender, recruitment and retention of faculty, funding for professional development, faculty workloads, evaluation, minority students, and ethics. These challenges have no quick fixes, and they can be met and dealt with only through the combined efforts of the entire academic leadership team, including the chief executive, the academic officer, deans, chairs, and faculty. The quality of leadership must be improved at all levels. Chairs should consider human resources, the structure of the organization, and political and symbolic frames of reference in providing leadership to the department. They must pay attention to upgrading leadership skills through mentoring, reading, workshops, self-assessment, and networking. Creating a professional development plan can assist chairs to identify needs, specify objectives, and design techniques for assessment.

ADVISORY BOARD

CONSULTING EDITORS

Sock-Foon C. MacDougall
Bowie State University

James L. Morrison
The University of North Carolina–Chapel Hill

Patricia Murrell
Memphis State University

Barbara S. Plakens
Iowa State University

Curt W. Reimann
National Institute of Standards and Technology

William Rittenberg
Michigan State University

Robert A. Scott
Ramapo College

Karen Spear
Fort Lewis College

John M. Swales
The University of Michigan

James J. Szablewicz
Mapp, Mapp & Klein, Attorneys at Law

Jo Taylor
Wayne State University

William G. Tierney
The Pennsylvania State University

Kathryn Towns
The Pennsylvania State University–Harrisburg

Reginald Wilson
American Council on Education

REVIEW PANEL

Charles Adams
University of Massachusetts–Amherst

Louis Albert
American Association for Higher Education

Richard Alfred
University of Michigan

Philip G. Altbach
State University of New York–Buffalo

Marilyn J. Amey
University of Kansas

Louis C. Attinasi, Jr.
University of Houston

Robert J. Barak
Iowa State Board of Regents

Alan Bayer
Virginia Polytechnic Institute and State University

John P. Bean
Indiana University

Louis W. Bender
Florida State University

John M. Braxton
Vanderbilt University

Peter McE. Buchanan
Council for Advancement and
    Support of Education

John A. Centra
Syracuse University

Arthur W. Chickering
George Mason University

Shirley M. Clark
Oregon State System of Higher Education

Darrel A. Clowes
Virginia Polytechnic Institute and State University

John W. Creswell
University of Nebraska–Lincoln

Deborah DiCroce
Piedmont Virginia Community College

Richard Duran
University of California

Kenneth C. Green
University of Southern California

Edward R. Hines
Illinois State University

Marsha W. Krotseng
West Virginia State College and University Systems

George D. Kuh
Indiana University–Bloomington

Daniel T. Layzell
University of Wisconsin System

Meredith Ludwig
American Association of State Colleges and Universities

Mantha V. Mehallis
Florida Atlantic University

Robert J. Menges
Northwestern University

Toby Milton
Essex Community College

James R. Mingle
State Higher Education Executive Officers

Gary Rhoades
University of Arizona

G. Jeremiah Ryan
Harford Community College

Mary Ann Sagaria
Ohio State University

Daryl G. Smith
Claremont Graduate School

William Tierney
The Pennsylvania State University

Susan Twombly
University of Kansas

Harold Wechsler
University of Rochester

Michael J. Worth
The George Washington University

CONTENTS

FOREWORD

Possibly the most important yet underrated position in a college or university is the department chair—the person in a position to have the most effective influence on the faculty but, for most institutions, the most neglected or least integrated position in the organizational structure.

The department chair is a relatively new position. It was not until the turn of the century that a few colleges, such as Harvard, became large enough, or specialized enough, to warrant separate units for different academic specialties. When they did, department faculties would elect one of their own to represent them to other academic units and the administration. This person, considered "first among equals," was to represent and protect the faculty's interests, not to be the first link in the administrative chain of authority. This attitude toward the primary role of the department chair continues.

In reality, the role of the department chair has changed dramatically. As institutions grew, so did the administrative need to have greater leadership and control below the dean. The logical frontline administrator was the department chair. While institutions were still small or specialized enough to have a clear, unifying vision, little conflict occurred. But as they grew and their sense of vision and purpose became less distinct, the aspirations of administrators increasingly came in conflict with those of faculty. External demands further complicated the role of the department chair.

The uncertainty over the performance of department chairs continues for three reasons. First is the confusion about role caused by the way chairs are selected. In many institutions, department chairs are selected for a finite term of office by faculty vote, after which they return to the faculty. For the outgoing department chair, this method creates strong loyalties to the faculty; for the faculty, it creates a chance to elect a person who will give them the least amount of grief; and for the person elected, the opportunity is often reluctantly accepted as "my turn in the barrel." When the chair is an administrative appointment with tenure, that person's loyalty is trapped between what the administration wants and the knowledge that someday he or she might become a colleague of those currently supervised. In either case, that link to the faculty sets up an expectation for the role that could conflict with the position's administrative responsibilities.

A second reason for the continued uncertainty can best be described by the psychological phrase, "learned helplessness," caused when the faculty and the chair are tenured and the department has a history of weak leadership. Tenure guarantees a lifetime faculty appointment, which, for the faculty, often means that they can wait out a disliked chair. If this attitude is part of the institutional culture, the administration might believe it has little direct influence over the faculty as long as the faculty performs to a minimal standard. Hence, both sides are in a state of learned helplessness—faculty as they wait out the administration, and administrators who feel that the existence of tenure prevents direct action.

The third condition is related to adequate training. In contrast to organizations that believe their most important resource is their employees and that the only way to ensure top performance is to provide continuous opportunities for training, most colleges and universities do not value the continuous training of their professional staff. Training for department chairs can be characterized as casual to nonexistent, oriented only toward understanding administrative procedures, and situational rather than holistic or systematic.

This report by Alan T. Seagren, professor of educational administration and of curriculum and instruction, John W. Creswell, professor of educational psychology, and Daniel W. Wheeler, coordinator of professional and organizational development, all at the University of Nebraska–Lincoln, looks at department chairs' role as leader and in faculty evaluation and development, the politics of chairing a department, and the influence of institutional type and academic discipline.

The conditions that contribute to the confusion and ineffectiveness of department chairs can be corrected without affecting the basic value of academic freedom. One proposed solution is to remove the departmental structure. Doing so might temporarily have a positive effect, but unless the fundamental conditions that contribute to the current confusion about roles and to the state of learned helplessness are corrected, these conditions will likely persist, regardless of organizational structure. This report will help institutions, schools, and departments better understand the position of the department chair and consequently provide a foundation for future action.

Jonathan D. Fife
Series Editor, Professor of Higher Education Administration, and Director, ERIC Clearinghouse on Higher Education

ACKNOWLEDGMENTS

The authors wish to acknowledge, with gratitude, the support, patience, and assistance of Jonathan Fife at the ERIC office at the George Washington University. Additionally, the authors are deeply indebted to the following contributing authors: Lindsay Barker, professor, University of Southern Queensland, Australia; Leon Cantrell, dean of the School of Arts, University of New England, Northern Rivers, New South Wales, Australia; Michael Miller, assistant professor, Teachers College, University of Nebraska–Lincoln; and David Carter, Methodist College, Omaha, Nebraska.

Special appreciation is due Phyllis Haase at the University of Nebraska–Lincoln for typing rough drafts, and to Marlene Starr and the staff of Teachers College Word Processing Center for their assistance and patience in programming the second draft and the final manuscript.

ROLES AND RESPONSIBILITIES OF THE CHAIR

Academic chairs[1] occupy a pivotal position in the organization of higher education. An estimated 80 percent of all university decisions are made at the departmental level (Roach 1976), and the position of department chair is the most common entry point into the hierarchy of academic administration (McDade 1987). "An institution can run for a long time with an inept president but not for long with inept chairpersons" (Peltason 1984, p. xi). As administrators responsible for evaluating and rewarding staff, chairs promote or inhibit the advancement of individual careers. As advocates for faculty, they serve as important communication links between academic units and the administrative hierarchy of colleges and universities. As colleagues of faculty and staff in the department, they understand the daily frustrations and concerns of individuals employed in higher education institutions. The chair remains the only official on campus who attempts to "interpret the department to the administration and the administration to the faculty" (Booth 1982, p. 4), otherwise referred to as the "swivel effect" (Caplow and McGee 1965), in which the chair is in the middle between allegiance to faculty and to the administration and the institution.

Much of the literature over the past 40 years has focused on understanding the distinctive role of the academic chair and the special challenges it brings to individuals in that role. This section first analyzes the academic structure in which chairs work, explores the role of the department chair and the international body of literature about chairing that has developed in the last four decades, and presents different perceptions of the role of chairs from scholars, chairs themselves, faculty in departments, and academic deans to whom chairs report. It concludes with a focus on conflict, transitions, and stress for chairs.

The Departmental Structure
As midlevel leaders in the academy, academic chairs hold academic or programmatic positions in units called college "divi-

"An institution can run for a long time with an inept president but not for long with inept chairpersons."

---

1. Reflecting the various types of schools and international customs, "leaders" of departments hold different titles. Out of respect for gender, many studies today use the term "chairperson" or its abbreviated version, "chair," for the leader of a department rather than the earlier "chairman." On some campuses, particularly in Australia and in Commonwealth countries, the individual is known as a "head," signifying a permanent position with administrative appointment. Occasionally, the individual is called a "department executive officer." This monograph uses the term "chair" for the most part.

---

sions," "colloquia," or, most frequently, "departments." Because the departmental structure is the most popular in colleges and universities, it is important to understand its evolution and the arguments both for and against its existence.

Academic departments in the United States date back to the 19th century (McHenry and Associates 1977). In the late 19th century, it became impossible for one tutor to teach a single class in all subjects (Anderson 1976). The emergence of new fields of study, the influence of professors trained in Germany, and the increasing specialization of education at the graduate level all contributed to the development of the current departmental structure in U.S. colleges and universities. The structure now consists of an academic unit led by an individual (the chair or head) comprised of faculty and support staff who engage in the multifaceted activities of an institution, such as providing courses for students, enhancing and developing scholarly knowledge, and providing service to the campus and the communities external to the institution.

The departmental structure, comprised of courses, programs of study, faculty, students, and support staff, has withstood many challenges and critics. *The Confidence Crisis,* for example, contends that academic departments inhibit the growth of new fields of knowledge, help isolate professors, and narrow courses and research in specialized areas (Dressel, Johnson, and Marcus 1971). Another author argues that departments thwart interdisciplinary efforts, resulting in faculty members' resistance to change in the curricula, requirements, and instructional practices (Corson 1975). Advocates for departments, however, suggest that they represent a vital organizational structure on campus. Faculty develop, preserve, and transmit knowledge through the departmental structure. Departments provide a "home" for faculty and students, serving as the nexus for close interaction with a minimum of misunderstanding and superfluous effort among themselves and providing an understandable and workable status system within which a faculty member can be oriented, professionally evaluated, and developed (Anderson 1976; Creswell et al. 1990). "It is at the department level that the real institutional business gets conducted" (Bennett 1983, p. 1).

The Importance of Chairing a Department
Chairs are important in the overall academic leadership team on campus that includes staff personnel, deans, vice presi-

dents or provosts, and chief executive officers. As early as 1942, the chair was characterized as the "key position" in a department and in the institution (Jennerich 1981). The first thorough study of department chairs was conducted in 1958 by surveying department chairs at 33 private liberal arts colleges (Jennerich 1981). An editorial in *The Journal of Higher Education* noted that "no one plays a larger part in determining the character of higher educational institutions than the department chairman" (Patton 1961, p. 459).

Department chairs make up possibly the largest administrative group in U.S. colleges and universities (Norton 1980). In 1981, the American Council on Education estimated that nearly 80,000 department chairs were involved in higher education (Scott 1981). Though the overall demographic structure of higher education institutions has changed since 1981, the number of changes might actually have grown in the last decade. In addition to the sizable number of midlevel administrators, one in three faculty serves in the post at some point during his or her career (Scott 1981).

The importance of chairing a department revolves around three highly interrelated factors. First, chairs have "daily contact" with administrators, faculty, and students (Weinberg 1984). In the administrative hierarchy of an institution, chairs oversee the department's daily operations. Chairs have been called the "single most important link" in the campus structure between administrators, faculty, programs, and students (Waltzer 1975, p. 5). This link serves as a conduit through which the intentions of top management flow down and information flows up. As such, chairs often serve as negotiators between departmental goals (reflecting institutional priorities) and individual goals.

Second, chairs are important decision makers.

Part of the uniqueness of the academic governance structure of a higher education institution is that the power for decision making lies at the bottom rather than at the top, that is, with the faculty rather than the academic officer. The faculty, either formally or through practice, makes decisions on curriculum structure, program offerings, hiring, promotion, and tenure, and, therefore, good leadership is imperative. This leadership is assigned to the program or department chair (Fife 1982, foreword).

And third, on most campuses the chair has the authority over matters important to the faculty and staff: curriculum, budget, faculty hiring, and evaluation (Bennett 1983; Carroll 1990). The chair is the "custodian of academic standards," charged with monitoring the departmental or divisional curriculum, seeing that course assignments are made judiciously and that individual faculty members' talents are aligned with instructional needs, promoting racial and gender balance in the faculty, encouraging continued personal and professional growth, and attesting to the adequacy of instruction and research (Bennett and Figuli 1990).

A chair's responsibilities have implications for the financial management of the institution. With fewer resources, the importance of the chair as the manager of departmental budgets is expected to increase (Bennett 1982). Chairs must consider approaches for allocating funds, awarding fair and equitable salaries, and using monies for incentives (Creswell et al. 1990), as well as reallocating departmental budgets, convincing staff to reduce their expenditures, negotiating deficits with senior administrators, and setting long-range fiscal goals for the unit. Other factors likely to focus attention on chairs are a high rate of job turnovers, the more precise roles and functions identified in collective bargaining contracts, and decreased mobility and morale among faculty and their implications for staffing (Bennett 1982).

The recent literature about department chairs helps to gauge the importance of chairs. The literature about chairing an academic unit has developed worldwide, especially in the 1980s, and includes doctoral dissertations, journal articles, a few monographs, and several books, some of which have been revised more than once (see, e.g., Bennett and Figuli 1990; Creswell et al. 1990; Jennerich 1981; Moses and Roe 1990; Tucker 1992). Several newsletters, in both English and foreign languages, are available for department chairs.[2]

---

2. See, e.g., *The Department Advisor,* published by Higher Education Executive Publications, Inc., in affiliation with the American Council on Education, Center for Leadership Development, Washington, D.C.; *The Department Chair,* published by Anker Publishing Company, Boston, Massachusetts; the *CSDC Newsletter,* published by Washington State University's Center for the Study of the Department Chair, supported by the University Council on Educational Administration; Brookes 1988; Kremer-Hayon and Avi-Izhak 1986; Lonsdale and Bardsley 1984; Schnell 1987; Startup 1976; Watson 1986.

Studies of the Chair's Role

In terms of roles and responsibilities, no administrator in the college and university setting has been analyzed as much as academic chairs. Since 1965, at least 12 studies have attempted to map those roles and responsibilities (see table 1), addressing the "tasks," "duties," "responsibilities," "activities," and "roles" of chairs. When roles were discussed, tasks and duties were grouped into larger, more encompassing domains (e.g., Smart and Elton 1976). The duties, tasks, or responsibilities in these studies range from a list of 27 (Smart and Elton 1976) to a list of 98 (Seagren 1978); roles include as few as two (e.g., McLaughlin, Montgomery, and Malpass 1975) to as many as 28 (e.g., Tucker 1984, 1992). A complex role emerges from these portraits, yet these role typologies seldom build on each other or provide a definitive list of areas of responsibility. Indeed, job descriptions, if available, provide little insight into a chair's roles (Roach 1976). Perhaps the diverse roles and responsibilities are endemic to the tasks of chairing about which writers express ambiguity and disagreement. Also reflected is the emergence of classifications and typologies from different perspectives: anecdotal accounts from institutional perspectives (e.g., Waltzer 1975), thoughts from participants in workshops (e.g., Tucker 1984), in-depth case studies (e.g., Bennett 1983), and empirical analyses (e.g., McLaughlin, Montgomery, and Malpass 1975; "Roles of Department Chairs" 1992). From these many role studies emerges a picture of the roles and responsibilities as constructed by chairs themselves, by deans and administrative superiors of chairs, and by faculty.

The chair's job has been characterized as a "militarist" who uses power, authority, resources, and sanctions to command; a "malcontent" who delegates, defers, decides slowly, and acts defensively; a "masochist" who nags others to get tasks done; a "mediator" who cajoles, pacifies, rewards, and tends to complicate matters; a "messiah" who exhorts, inspires, and shames; and a "mentor" who leads with maturity, wisdom, and skill (Jacobs 1986). Typologies of a chair's role involve administrative leadership, program development, personnel development, and public relations (see, e.g., Bragg 1981; McLaughlin, Montgomery, and Malpass 1975; "Roles of Department Chairs" 1992; Seagren 1978; Seagren and Filan 1992).

A survey of 1,198 chairs at 38 state universities, rating how much time chairs spent and the enjoyment they received from

TABLE 1

STUDIES ABOUT THE ROLES AND RESPONSIBILITIES OF CHAIRS

Author	Focus	Aspect of Role/ Responsibility Examined	Specific Roles and Responsibilities
Norton 1980	Responsibilities in a college of education	8 task areas	Internal administration, budgetary planning, personnel administration & communication, curriculum, student personnel, personal & professional development
Bragg 1981	Subroles emphasized by chairs	Faculty-, externally, program-, management-oriented	Recruiting, evaluation, negotiation, enhancement of department's image, program development
Jennerich 1981	Competencies of chairs	14 skills and competencies	Character/integrity, leadership ability, interpersonal ability, communication, decision making, organization
Tucker 1984, 1992	Diversity of roles	28 possible roles	Governance of department, instruction, faculty affairs, student affairs, external communication, budget & resources, office management, professional development
Moses & Roe 1990	Headship functions	40 functions	Staff & student affairs, professional development, administration, one's own academic activities, budget & resources
"Roles of Department Chairs" 1992	Roles	Leader, scholar, faculty developer & manager	Elements identified for each role
Seagren & Filan 1992	Roles, tasks, competencies	18 roles, 32 tasks, 12 competencies	E.g., motivator, integrate unit plans, decisiveness

these roles, found department chairs played three major roles—academic, administrative, and leadership (McLaughlin, Montgomery, and Malpass 1975). The chairs felt most comfortable with the academic role, which involved duties associated with teaching, advising, conducting and encouraging research, developing curriculum, and faculty development and related activities (corroborated by Boice and Myers 1986). Chairs reported that they spent almost half of their time teaching, advising, or engaging in research. The administrative role involved duties within the department: maintaining records, administering the budget, managing staff employees, and the like. Respondents believed that time spent on this role was beyond their control, and they appeared to derive little enjoyment from it. The leadership role (discussed in greater detail in the following section) included providing leadership for departmental faculty and program development. The effort the chairs spent on this role was related to the size of the department and to the amount of enjoyment they derived from it.

Another study, of 39 department heads from nine colleges within a single major university, examined how chairs learn their roles through socializing experiences (Bragg 1981). The study found that chairs tend to emphasize one role more than others in their work. "Faculty-oriented" heads described their primary responsibilities as recruiting, developing, and evaluating faculty members, facilitating the work of the faculty, and reducing intradepartmental conflict to improve the faculty's morale (see the section titled "The Role of the Chair in Faculty Evaluation and Development" for more detail). "Externally oriented" heads described their primary roles as representers, brokers, negotiators, and grantsmen. "Management-oriented" heads were focused on administrative responsibilities for the academic department, and "program-oriented" heads engaged primarily in program development. The study further identified for each role the chairs' goals when they were appointed, their sources of stress, and the importance of extradepartmental involvement.

Yet another study, in a different tack, explored chairs' perceptions of their effectiveness to discover roles ("Roles of Department Chairs" 1992). In fall 1991, 800 department chairs in 100 research and doctorate-granting institutions were asked how effective they felt they were on 26 duties. From those duties, investigators statistically derived four roles: leader, scholar, faculty developer, and manager. Next, chairs that reported their effectiveness in the top quartile were compared with those reporting in the lower three quartiles in terms of personal, organizational, positional, and productivity variables for the four roles. The most effective "scholars" were most productive as researchers and experienced significantly less role conflict than other chairs. Those who felt they were effective "faculty developers" were more likely to accept additional terms as chairs and to be in departments with a greater proportion of nontenured faculty than other chairs. Chairs who saw themselves as effective "leaders" also saw themselves as effective "managers," and effective leader-managers were more inclined to view themselves as faculty and administrators than other chairs.

Recently, the Center for the Study of Higher and Postsecondary Education of the University of Nebraska–Lincoln, the Maricopa Community College, and the National Academy for Community College Chairs undertook a national study of chairs in all two-year colleges in the United States and Canada (Seagren and Filan 1992). The authors designed questions to determine the broader roles of chairs, the specific activities in their work, and the overall competencies required for their position. An overriding conceptual model directed the design: a model of department chairs' careers based on personal characteristics, educational beliefs and values, job dimensions, job challenges, and response strategies. The roles of chairs were conceptualized by 18 dimensions resulting from preliminary studies of chairs in four-year schools (Creswell et al. 1990) and identified role metaphors (Creswell and Brown 1992; Tucker 1984, 1992). Respondents were asked to indicate the relative importance of 18 roles, such as "motivator" and "caretaker," and 32 tasks, which represented a revision of the 54 dimensions (Tucker 1984, 1992) and the 98 tasks (Seagren 1978) identified earlier. The tasks represented specific responsibilities, such as "seek external funding," "promote affirmative action," and "integrate unit plans with institutional plans." The investigators designed questions to explore chairs' competencies, using the 12 skills mentioned in the Assessment Center Project of the National Association of Secondary School Principals (Wendel and Sybouts 1988) and forming questions about components of each skill, such as "Problem analysis—ability to seek out relevant data" or "Decisiveness—ability to recognize when a decision is required." Thus, the Nebraska Project used three methods to explore the roles, tasks, and skills of chairs within the population of chairs at two-year community colleges.

A survey of heads of departments or schools and of staff in nine universities in Australia (Moses and Roe 1990) contained 40 functions of heads. Heads were asked to respond on a scale for both importance and enjoyment and to indicate items rated as important but neglected because of the lack of time. Sixty percent or more of the heads regarded 21 items as of great importance, which were then grouped into the

categories of staff and student affairs, professional development for staff, administrative items, the chair's own academic
activities, legal activities, and resources. Fifty percent or more
of the heads enjoyed 15 functions, and 20 percent or more
of the heads disliked nine functions. The top four functions
for which heads needed more time were four of the top five
functions that heads enjoyed. In general, the more routine
aspects of administrative and legal affairs and resource allocation were seen as less important than staff and student
affairs and professional development for staff and considerably
less enjoyable than planning one's own academic activity.

An extensive list of actual activities and tasks organizes 54
duties into eight areas (Tucker 1984, 1992): departmental governance (e.g., conduct departmental meetings), instruction
(e.g., schedule classes), faculty affairs (e.g., recruit and select
faculty members), student affairs (e.g., advise students), external communication (e.g., improve and maintain the department's image and reputation), budget and resources (e.g.,
seek outside funding), office management (e.g., monitor
building security and maintenance), and professional development (e.g., stimulate faculty research and publication). A
further perspective about how chairs view their role was provided in an observational study of one chair (the chair of the
Department of Educational Administration and Supervision)
in a major research university (Seedorf and Gmelch 1989).
Observations of this individual identified five dimensions of
work: attendance at scheduled meetings, attendance at
unscheduled meetings, phone calls, tours (leaving the office
to visit with others), and desk work. The study revealed that
scheduled meetings consumed almost half the day (47 percent), followed by unscheduled meetings (22 percent), and
desk work (15 percent). The least amount of time was spent
on tours (9 percent) and phone calls (6 percent).

Fewer observations (and certainly fewer studies) focus on
the role of chairs as seen by faculty and administrators to
whom they report. Faculty see chairs largely as advocates and
as allocating resources to meet their needs. In one study, faculty stressed the role of chairs as giving encouragement; the
staff wanted department heads to encourage good teaching
and to stimulate research and publication, taking into account
each staff member's special talents and interests (Moses 1984).
A national study of faculty members' ratings of 458 chairs

found that faculty wanted chairs oriented toward both structure (tasks) and relationships (Knight and Holen 1985).

The role of the chair as seen by deans relates primarily to the dean, the institution, and effective communication (Jeffrey 1985; Warren 1990). From the dean's perspective, a chair might have six roles relating to the total organization:

- Conveying to the faculty that the dean is accessible, a dependable source of information, and a partner with faculty and staff;
- Relaying information expeditiously to individuals in the department;
- Promptly and clearly communicating data from the department to the dean;
- Communicating to the staff a clear grasp of the institution's mission and objectives;
- Planning and periodically assessing objectives for the department and for individual faculty;
- "Biting the bullet" on difficult decisions and issues rather than relying solely on the dean (Warren 1990).

Chairs should focus their attention on representing the department not only to the college, but also to the university, to the interinstitutional academic scene, and to the public (Henry 1974). Likewise, chairs need to represent the college administration to the department, a task "not always popular, pleasant, or easy" (p. 1). They need to provide analysis, options, and alternatives in the most important arena: the selection and advancement of personnel. Chairs should not let their unit drift; they should keep alive questions about the department's agenda, especially items related to program planning and effective performance (Henry 1974).

Conflicts, Ambiguities, and Transitions

The multifaceted roles of chairs are embedded within a larger context of demands by diverse groups. Not surprisingly, the literature on chairs speaks to the conflicts and ambiguities of individuals moving into or holding positions as chairs. The literature explores five interrelated areas: the multiple expectations of others for chairs, the ambiguous mandate of the office, the unclear lines of authority, transitional issues of the role of faculty-chair, and the stresses that accompany the position.

Like other administrators or leaders in higher education, chairs face many demands and expectations from individuals who have a stake in the operation of an academic unit—central administration, faculty, and students among them (Pappas 1989). Students often seek a voice in the number of required courses and the requirements of majors and degrees, faculty want to increase requirements, and alumni voice concern over the laxness of courses (Tucker 1984). College deans, central administrators, and professional accrediting agencies also seek a voice. The chair thus becomes a "fulcrum in the balancing act" (Tucker 1984, p. 6) among these contending forces.

This fulcrum has no clear pivot point, however. Chairs suffer from role ambiguity because they have no clear mandate for their position. They seldom are supplied with clear job descriptions or clear criteria for performing their jobs. They come to the position without training (Waltzer 1975), though they might have experience in quasi-administrative roles (such as chairing an important departmental committee) before assuming the responsibilities of a chair (Creswell et al. 1990). Unfortunately, a chair's experiences before taking the position seldom include any formal orientation (see, e.g, Bragg 1981).

Chairs, like the god Janus, have two faces: an administrator and a faculty member.

Chairs, like the god Janus, have two faces: an administrator and a faculty member (Gmelch and Burns 1991). The conflicts for chairs include resolving tensions both horizontally (for the department) and vertically (for the institution) (Brown 1977). Because chairs must represent both faculty and administrative perspectives, this in-between status raises questions about how they should act and be perceived. Perhaps chairs should assume one of three views toward their role and position:

- They are really just another faculty member who happens temporarily to have additional and somewhat different duties and who identifies with departmental colleagues as the real constituency and object of loyalty.
- They have changed in some basic way by becoming an extension of the college administration and view the administration as their key constituency.
- They have a representative view of the discipline and receive the mandate to lead from the discipline itself instead of from departmental colleagues or administration (Bennett 1982).

Though in all probability no single view characterizes all of the ways chairs behave, these three views represent the ambiguity in the role of a chair and chairs' use of elaborate strategies to protect themselves from faculty stake holders. Chairs express little interest in the position to their faculty colleagues and develop a litany of disclaimers—statements that they have only reluctantly accepted the responsibilities, dismay at being separated from their first loves of teaching and research, and reluctance to admit that the job is both enjoyable and honorable (Bennett 1982).

The organizational and individual context in which chairing occurs affects the ambiguity and strains of the position. As individuals who are neither "pure faculty nor regular administration" (Bennett 1982, p. 54), chairs operate within an organizational, departmental structure that is based on the academic model of faculty autonomy in decision making and peer control over departmental life (Booth 1982). Although the authority of faculty varies by type of institution (Birnbaum 1988), such authority can cause conflict with the administrative model of efficiency and the top-down pattern of decision making.

Inherent in the job of chairing a department is the potential conflict between faculty and administrative views of the department chair (figure 1). The administrative view (the top circle) of training, evaluation, feedback, and quality of performance for department chairs is driven by expectations as defined by the administration and the chair's perception of responsibilities. This view could conflict with a faculty member's view (the lower circle) of a department chair, whose expectations in being elected or appointed flow from the faculty. These expectations in turn affect the chair's perceptions of responsibilities. From a faculty member's perspective, training, evaluation, feedback, and quality of performance should flow from faculty-defined expectations. Thus, the administrative view and the faculty view of the chair often conflict.

Individual professional goals, multiple institutional expectations, an ambiguous mandate, and unclear lines of authority all apply pressure to individuals upwardly mobile on the career path to a chair position. The typical career path for a department chair begins within an academic discipline as a graduate student, then faculty in the same discipline, moving up through faculty ranks and eventually becoming the depart-

FIGURE 1

THE DEPARTMENT CHAIR'S DILEMMA

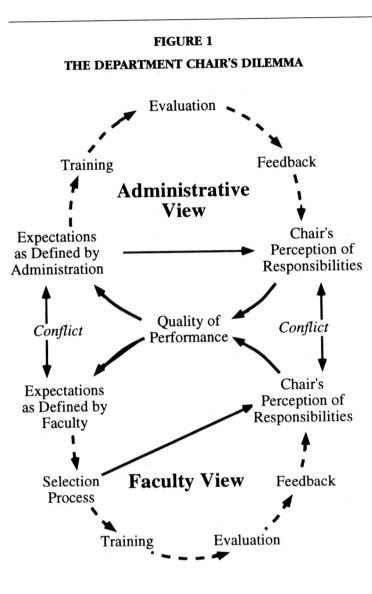

Source: Faculty Senate Committee, the George Washington University.

ment chair (Carroll 1990). Stepping into the role of chair occurs when faculty are in their middle to upper 40s (i.e., 46 in Carroll 1990 and 48 in Boice and Myers 1986). Chairs serve for about six years, and 65 percent return to faculty status immediately after their service (Carroll 1990). Female chairs are significantly younger than their male counterparts when they take the position and are more likely to become a department chair before receiving full professorship than males (Carroll 1990).

Whether female or male, individuals assuming the position of chair experience abrupt changes in their work life, adding to the strains and stresses of academic life. Facing these diverse roles is difficult, given the fact that chairs come out of the ranks of faculty in disciplines that might be far afield from management or leadership. They change from work that is solitary (as a faculty member) to more social (as a chair), from focused activities to fragmented ones, from being autonomous to being accountable to others, from being manuscript-oriented to being memo-oriented, from being private to being public, from being professional to being conscious of public relations, from being stable within a discipline and circle of professional associations to being mobile within the university structure and among chairs at other universities and colleges, from requesting resources to being a custodian of and dispensing resources, and from practicing austerity with little control over one's resources to enjoying more control (Gmelch 1989).

The transformation to the position of chair undoubtedly is stressful and presages the stress of the position itself. A national study of 800 department chairs in research and doctorate-granting schools (Gmelch 1991) found the leading stressors to be the time needed for administrative duties, confrontations with colleagues, pressures to keep current in one's discipline, and job demands' interfering with personal time. Having a workload that was too heavy headed the list of leading stressors (59 percent complained about the problem; see also Mitchell 1987). Workload in Gmelch's study was defined as the desirability to spend time on activities, not the total number of hours. In fact, chairs and professors worked approximately the same number of hours per week (56 and 52, respectively), but chairs simply spent time on activities they did not want to spend time on (completing paperwork, attending meetings, dealing with rules and regulations).

To cope with the stresses of being chair, individuals deal directly with the problems, turn to recreation, avoid problems, talk to friends, talk about the problems, and reframe or re-structure their thinking (Boice and Myers 1986). They are advised to manage the work environment better by identifying high payoff activities and developing a more efficient system for handling paperwork, view rules as boundaries rather than rigid guidelines, and protect their time to maintain academic productivity (Gmelch 1991). Although these strategies might not lighten the burden of an ambiguous role and the strains accompanying it, they offer useful advice for faculty in transition to a role as chair as well as for more experienced chairs.

THE CHAIR'S ROLE AS LEADER

This section identifies specific aspects of the theory and practice of leadership most relevant to the work of a department chair and suggests several ways for chairs to acquire and implement the necessary skills and techniques.

Leadership and the Chair

A leader is an individual who directs and guides the organization to its highest levels of achievement (Yukl 1989), and "leadership" is perhaps the most widely used word in the literature dealing with the management and administration of organizations. Much of the discussion and research on leadership come from the application of theories derived from social psychology and business administration (Bennis and Nanus 1985; Kotter 1988; Luthans, Hodgetts, and Rosenkrantz 1988; Yukl 1989).

Numerous accounts of higher education in the United States, from the highly critical to the self-congratulatory, invoke the absence of leadership as the cause of higher education's perceived ills or the abundance of leadership as the reason for its apparent successes (Rosovsky 1990). Literature dealing with the university presidency, in particular, often stresses the exercise of leadership as the crucial factor leading to an institution's success (Cohen and March 1986; Kerr 1984), but vice presidents and deans are also seen as leaders with key roles in an institution's success (Cameron and Ulrich 1986; Tucker and Bryan 1988).

Less attention is given to the leadership role of the academic chair, though its importance has not been denied (Brown, Scott, and Winner 1987). Only recently has the literature on leadership in higher education recognized that the standing of an academic institution in large part is a measure of the standing of its individual departments (Bennett and Figuli 1990; Knight and Holen 1985). Little has been added to the literature focused on leadership by department chairs since Tucker's *Chairing the Academic Department* first appeared more than a decade ago.

More recent accounts of the role and work of chairs concentrate on the range of chairs' tasks and on the skills needed for effective implementation (Bennett and Figuli 1990; Creswell et al. 1990), emphasizing the administration rather than the leadership of departments. Beyond a doubt, however, the chairs of academic departments are key leaders in any successful higher education institution, and, without such leadership by chairs, no institution can be continuously successful. The most lauded university president is not an isolated figure in an organization but a leader of leaders, and, with the growing complexities of institutional and departmental management, this statement is even more true today then ever before (Bensimon, Neumann, and Birnbaum 1989; Birnbaum 1988; Cameron and Ulrich 1986; Rosovsky 1990; Tucker 1984).

Defining Leadership

What is leadership? Is it possible to apply theories of leadership to the situations and challenges that department chairs face? To answer these questions, it is first necessary to examine some current theories of leadership and to test their relevance to higher education institutions. For purposes of this section, theories of leadership can be divided into three groups: natural leaders, organizational behavior, and organizational environment.

The group with the longest tradition of research stems from the notion that some people are natural leaders. The theory seeks to define leadership in terms of the behavior or traits of those who are in positions of leadership (Yukl 1989), often mentioning qualities like ambition, assertiveness, the ability to make decisions, adaptability, self-confidence, vision, and the ability to articulate a vision. The most current research suggests that, while the existence of certain traits is likely to increase a leader's effectiveness, no guarantees can be made (Luthans 1992; Yukl 1989).

Two more sophisticated versions of the theory of traits emphasize contingency (Vroom 1983) and leaders' cognitive ability (Yukl 1989). The former stresses the way in which the organizational environment impinges on the relationship between the traits of leadership and the leader's effectiveness. The latter, cognitive resource theory, is particularly relevant to higher education institutions. Underlined in cognitive theory is the need to understand the relationship between the leader's qualities and experience and the group's. For a high-ability group, a nondirective leader is predicted to be more effective than a directive or autocratic leader (Bensimon, Neumann, and Birnbaum 1989; Birnbaum 1988).

The second group of leadership theories emphasizes the behavior of the group and sees leadership in terms of its effect on the behavior and perceptions of others. Research in this area focuses on a leader's apparent success or effectiveness in dealing with others and modifying the behavior of followers (Gardner 1990). In an organization like a college, where decision making by a group is often a valued means of sharing knowledge and perceptions, the leader can play a significant role in determining the group's effectiveness. Such a role will be difficult to achieve, however, if the group is unable to see the leader as one of its members (Birnbaum 1988; Yukl 1989).

A third group of theories emphasizes organizational environment and sees leadership as contingent upon and a response to appropriate and necessary circumstances. These theories deemphasize the behavior of leaders and groups, stressing instead the importance of the situation and the interaction between social, cultural, and political forces, and the leader and the organization (Yukl 1989). They emphasize the dynamic aspects of leadership and the need to ensure appropriate environmental monitoring. Theories of transformational leadership describe how a leader guides an organization or group through a period of change or transformation. The relevance of such theories to department chairs has only just begun to be determined (Bolman and Deal 1991; Cameron and Ulrich 1986).

All of these perspectives bear on the department chair's role as leader. Indeed, a number of important similarities draw aspects of the theories together. For example, almost all theories of leadership stress the importance of the leader's developing and maintaining effective relationships within the group (Kouzes and Posner 1987), for leaders need to know and understand those with whom they work. The theories also share a concern with the need for leaders to gather and use information, both from inside and outside the group, and to maintain appropriate lines of communication to these sources of information. Information enables a leader to determine relevant factors and to rank alternatives in order of importance. The importance of the involvement of those affected in decision making and the need to influence people by motivating them or by winning their support are other common factors. Thus, leaders need to learn a clearly defined set of skills or techniques (Fisher 1987; Kouzes and Posner 1987; Luthans 1992; Yukl 1989).

The literature on leadership also emphasizes that leaders have the capacity to articulate a vision or goal for the future and the tenacity to make that vision a reality, an especially important point in transformational theory (Bennis and Nanus 1985; Bolman and Deal 1991; Burns 1978). Vision is the means by which a chair can create a focus or agenda for the department's current and future plans. The chair does not invent a vision and then attempt to impose it on disbelieving colleagues; rather, the chair facilitates the debate and discussion through which the department clarifies its options and becomes aware of its possibilities. The chair then oversees the strategies by which those fragments of a future are crystallized into a shared set of goals and a plan by which to reach them (see, e.g., Moxley and Olson 1988).

Research on Leadership in Higher Education
The literature on leadership in higher education is derived from these more general theories of leadership, usually emphasizing the behavior or traits of the leader (Dill and Fullagar 1987). Successful academic leaders, in addition to their professional credibility, display certain characteristics, such as vigor, decisiveness, and a willingness to take chances. They are able to articulate a vision for their institution, thereby creating a focus and direction for the organization's efforts. They are able to persuade others to share their vision and to join in the task of translating intention into reality (Cameron and Ulrich 1986; Maxcy 1991).

Recent writings stress that the environmental context of leadership in colleges and universities varies significantly from institution to institution (Chaffee and Tierney 1988). This approach sees leadership as most successful when the leader recognizes the type or style of institution and adjusts strategies of leadership accordingly. For example, a large university with an essentially bureaucratic structure of governance needs a style of leadership different from a liberal arts college with a long tradition of collegial decision making, where the model of a leader as the "first among equals" might well be dominant (Bensimon, Neumann, and Birnbaum 1989; Birnbaum 1988).

Another theme in the literature draws attention to the ways in which higher education institutions differ from business and other organizations. The demands on leaders in public or not-for-profit organizations are exacerbated because public organizations often have diverse and conflicting goals (Pfeffer 1981), and leaders in higher education work within structures that are significantly different from those in other organizations (Vroom 1983). Typologies of management styles in colleges stress that the environment of higher education leadership is a much more shared phenomenon than in most enterprises that focus on profit. Indeed, many faculty expect to be advised, if not consulted, before the chair makes a major decision (Bensimon, Neumann, and Birnbaum 1989; McHenry and Associates 1977; Moomaw 1984).

Equally important, a faculty member might be an internationally recognized leader in a particular discipline and, as such, have a leadership role and agenda different from that of the department chair or even the president. Another faculty member might exercise a similarly substantial but informal and nondisciplinary role as leader within the organization.

In such a system, the "official" leaders, from the president down, operate on the tacit understanding that their legitimate spheres of authority and power exist side by side with those of others. The ability of the formal office holders to exercise leadership depends upon the ongoing support or compliance of those other leaders and of those others who are being led. In such a situation, the leadership roles of those in formal positions of organizational authority could more appropriately be seen as those who facilitate or empower rather than as those who control (Bensimon, Neumann, and Birnbaum 1989; Birnbaum 1988), especially in research universities and elite liberal arts colleges (Creswell et al. 1990).

How well do these theories fit with the limited research dealing with leadership and the department chair? As in the literature on the general issue of leadership in higher education, the successful chair's style or behavior of leadership is the most commonly discussed topic. Successful chairs have been described as having good interpersonal communication skills and as being concerned about others and good listeners. They are seen as having high academic credibility and are often chosen on the basis of their achievements in research and teaching (Creswell et al. 1990).

The literature also addresses the nature and state of the department over which the leadership is exercised. Chairs are advised to ensure as good a match as possible between the department's situation and needs and their own behavior as a leader. Particular strategies of leadership that might be appropriate and effective in one department might be highly inappropriate and unsuccessful in another (Groner 1978). Chairs should also address individual faculty members' career

The demands on leaders in public or not-for-profit organizations are exacerbated because public organizations often have diverse and conflicting goals. . . .

needs, some of whom might be less experienced than others (Bensimon, Neumann, and Birnbaum 1989).

The chair's ambiguous role is further emphasized. Is the chair the leader representing the faculty to the more senior administration, or vice versa? Many faculty see their department's leader as the person to blame if things go wrong or if the budget is cut. Others believe that the chair's role is to advance the faculty's individual self-interests and that the chair is to be replaced if it does not happen (Bennett 1988; Falk 1979).

The literature makes little attempt to match the various duties and responsibilities of the chair with specific strategies for developing and implementing leadership. The literature assumes that the administration of a department is its leadership and that the appointment of a chair will automatically provide a leader. But experience indicates that it is not always the case (Eble 1990a).

Exercising Leadership in the Department

An assumption of this section is that chairs are appointed or elected on the basis of their capacity to provide leadership in a disciplinary group, a group that varies in nature from discipline to discipline and from institution to institution. Leaders' interests and styles also differ from chair to chair, and the requirements of leadership vary according to a department's current place in its cycle of overall development and its relation to the model of governance at a particular institution (Birnbaum 1988).

Some chairs might be called upon to implement academic leadership of a high order in matters such as faculty and student recruitment, budget and financial planning, decisions about tenure, faculty development programs, the development and introduction of new programs, or a major revision of existing courses or assessment practices. Other chairs might see administrative leadership as more important, and still other chairs might be required to display skills in social, moral, or ethical leadership under difficult circumstances. Research into leadership in the University of California system stresses the importance of planning, resource management, and evaluation at all levels of institutional leadership (McCorkle and Archibald 1982). Increased public scrutiny of higher education and growing calls for greater accountability emphasize the need for leadership from department chairs more than ever before (Bennett and Figuli 1990; Creswell et al. 1990).

What leadership skills do department chairs need, and in what situations should these skills be used? The most obvious place for a department chair to exercise leadership is during faculty meetings. The chair often has control of the agenda for such meetings and the responsibility for ensuring the presentation and scrutiny of a variety of facts and opinions. The chair permits others to speak or respond and is ultimately accountable for preparing and distributing accurate accounts of what was said and done. Leadership of a faculty meeting is public, formal, and open to the scrutiny of all participants. Effective faculty meetings require excellent communication skills and well-developed strategies for preparation and follow-through. Skillful dealings with people are necessary to encourage participation and shared goals as well as to resolve conflicts (Eble 1990b).

Leadership of an academic department is carried on in many venues other than a faculty meeting, however. The chair's office, for instance, is the site where decisions are made and implemented daily. Access to information or informal discussions with faculty or students frequently require the exercise of the chair's responsibility and authority to act so as to overcome a problem or to seize an opportunity (Creswell et al. 1990).

Chairs also exercise their leadership in many locations beyond the department. They are responsible to a dean or academic vice president with whom they coordinate the overall leadership of the college or school. They often find a venue such as a dean's committee valuable for two additional reasons: It provides an opportunity for comparing their own performance and experience against those of other chairs, and it serves as a forum for the exchange of ideas and information about the daily routine of an educational leader. Experienced chairs can act as mentors for newcomers.

Chairs might also find that the institution and the broader community see them as the leader and representative of their discipline or department on every possible issue. They can be called upon to speak to a student gathering concerning a dispute over the status of an individual or an item of assessment. Local newspapers might contact them for comments about a development in their discipline or an incident far away. They almost certainly will address outside groups who regard them as acknowledged leaders, capable of providing further leadership to such a gathering.

Developing Skills as a Leader

Much of the research on leadership focuses on a single question: How do successful leaders acquire their skills of leadership? Some researchers have continued to argue that leaders are born, not made, but many organizations, though not many colleges and universities, spend a large part of their professional development funds to facilitate the growth and development of leaders on their staffs (Fisher 1987). A number of research centers and institutes have been established to investigate further the nature and origin of leadership (Clark and Freeman 1990; Tucker 1984).

The evidence suggests that leaders learn about leadership in several major ways: through the accumulation of experience that allows the establishment of a base of knowledge and precedent; through trial and error in which current leaders' success is a product of learned responses and reflection on earlier similar experiences; through other people whose performance as leaders provides a continuous source of ideas, information, and examples; through role models or mentors; or through education and training, especially in skills associated with dealing with people, communication, and strategic and lateral thinking (Yukl 1989).

The Goal of Departmental Leadership

What is the goal of leaders in higher education? What ends does the leader of an academic department seek? Most people wish to see higher education institutions well run, efficient, and accountable, as pleasant and stimulating places where one can work and study. Departments that are well led could be in a stronger position to compete for limited resources, top-quality students, and new faculty, and successful department chairs might be able to seek other positions of leadership at higher organizational levels.

The primary goal of a successful department leader, however, is to assist faculty and students to develop their disciplinary skills and experience to the best of their ability. This concept, the strengthening or empowering of others, is related to the long-standing tradition of individual academic autonomy, requiring the chair to develop a vision beyond immediate tasks and challenges toward longer-term aims and achievements. Such transformational leadership is essential if higher education is to cope with the challenges it currently faces (Cameron and Ulrich 1986). The leader's responsibility is then to ensure that the work load of each member of the department is designed to strengthen his or her professional status through the achievement of the shared vision. Only through such achievement can the standing of the individual, the department, the chair, and the institution be seen to have grown through leadership. Department chairs, arguably more than any other leader in higher education, are best able to work with individuals toward these shared goals (Bennett 1988).

Strategies for the Development of Leaders

Little published research relates to the precise ways in which department chairs exhibit and perform leadership, but the available evidence suggests some guidelines. A study of the process of transformational leadership in two higher education institutions identifies five steps that such leaders use: creating a need for change, overcoming resistance to change, articulating a vision, generating commitment, and implementing the vision (Cameron and Ulrich 1986). Useful for virtually all chairs is the focus on assisting a department to develop a clear vision for its future. Such a vision needs to accommodate likely realities as well as aspirations and achievable goals. The vision often originates with the chair but needs to be crystallized through departmental discussion and debate. The vision should be expressed in terms indicating the faculty's ownership of and commitment to its achievement.

A second strategy of leadership that successful chairs have used is to ensure that effective data bases are available to provide information necessary for informed decision making, especially in relation to impending change (Creswell et al. 1990). Professional journals and associations, networks, the higher education press, employers of graduates, government papers and reports, the media, alumni, colleagues, and students are all potential sources of information that could be vital in articulating or refining a goal. Many of the notices and items that reach a chair's desk are of interest and relevance to all department faculty. Information passed along will provide faculty with a constant stream of material that can be used to enhance their own professional standing and to strengthen their commitment to the shared vision.

A third strategy of interest to chairs who want to lead their departments to positions of excellence is an understanding of the dynamics and politics of the institution. Chairs need to monitor and observe that broader stage on which the realities of departmental visions will be played out (Minter 1990). A chair who is constantly rebuffed at the dean's door will find faculty support and enthusiasm beginning to wane, however splendid the vision. (The next section provides additional information on how a chair might gain skills in working through the system.)

The research on leadership in other organizations is also useful, and corporate-based research in particular can provide useful insights into leadership in higher education (Dill and Fullagar 1987). "Total quality management" espoused by W. Edwards Deming (1982) emphasizes the importance of developing a vision that can be understood and shared by employees and customers alike. The role of the leader in overseeing the implementation of the vision and of monitoring its progress is also important. Such leaders have been shown to draw upon their fund of credibility to elicit initial support and then to strengthen their position through effective and regular communication with all key personnel (Sherr and Teeter 1991). The revitalization of the Ford Motor Company in the 1980s, for example, is partly the result of an emphasis on leaders as agents and facilitators of change rather than as experts and controllers (Pascale 1990).

Summary

Department chairs in colleges and universities might feel somewhat distant from the boardrooms and executive suites of large corporations. But they face challenges of and opportunities for leadership not unlike those confronting the managers of industry and commerce. They are subject to a similar range and diversity of internal and external environmental pressures and are just as stretched between what seems necessary and what is possible.

This section has identified diverse styles of leadership and roles, and common traits that are likely to be of assistance and relevance to the chair's tasks. It has demonstrated particular ways in which the chair, placed in an organization centered on disciplinary strengths and allegiances, can win support and assistance for the pursuit of a shared goal. The principal aim of departmental leadership is to enhance academic excellence through the professional empowerment of all those faculty and students for whom the chair is responsible.

Colleges and universities are complex, loosely coupled organizations that are very difficult to manage by traditional centralist models of management. They are not comparable to business corporations, which are created to provide goods and services for profit (Birnbaum 1988). The goals successful businesses set and attain and the processes they use are usually clear and can be described precisely.

Universities do not exhibit these characteristics. They serve clients whose needs are ambiguous, have highly professional staffs who expect to have a substantial say in decision making (Mintzberg 1979), and use teaching methods and research processes that cannot be described precisely—all characteristic of organizations whose context for work displays a high degree of uncertainty. This uncertainty provides an environment in which political behavior is likely to be used to influence others (Pfeffer, Salanick, and Leblebici 1976), and in professional organizations, political activity is a much more likely response to scarce resources and dissensus than in others (Welsh and Slusher 1986). Throughout the history of higher education, scarce resources and dissensus have loomed as major components of the university environment, helping to ensure that, for department chairs, politics is an inescapable fact of life.

Colleges and Universities as Political Organizations

None of the theoretical models of organizational decision making fit perfectly the politically charged, ambiguous environment of higher education, but the Political Model (Baldridge 1971b) and the Organized Anarchy Model (Cohen and March 1986) both provide useful insights into how institutions work. The Political Model contends that colleges and universities work as political systems in which the driving force is to a large extent derived from group dynamics, while the Organized Anarchy Model is applicable when ambiguous goals, unclear processes, and fluid participation by the organization's members are apparent. The Organized Anarchy Model focuses on nonpurposive behavior and postulates almost completely random decision making; the extent to which it adequately describes college and university decision making is not clear, and it has been suggested that it applies only to peripheral decision making in these organizations (Hardy et al. 1984).

Applying these two models to colleges and universities suggests that, for purposes of analysis, these organizations can be seen as political organizations in which conflict is a natural state (Davies and Morgan 1982; Gessner 1988). Colleges and universities are organized anarchies to the extent that they exhibit decision making that is at least to some extent shaped by ambiguous goals, rewards, and sanctions, and a high degree of authority and autonomy by subordinates. Further, such organizations are political systems to the extent that they are sites of ongoing power struggles involving individuals, loose groupings, and coalitions all seeking to maximize their autonomy and control (Bacharach and Lawler 1980; Collins 1975, 1979; Welsh and Slusher 1986).

The state of higher education's culture is not to suggest that politics is inherently evil, despite the long and lingering influence of Machiavelli's *The Prince*. Politics as a behavioral concept is morally neutral, but the tactics of politics can be misused for immoral purposes if individuals employ inappropriate means to gain desired ends.

Politics of the Organization

Politics provides an avenue, often the only avenue, through which conflicting opinions within the department can be reconciled. "Organizational politics involves those activities taken within organizations to acquire, develop, and use power and other resources to obtain one's preferred outcomes in a situation where there is dissensus about choices" (Pfeffer 1981, p. 7). Chairs must therefore be politically active and must make sure that they are seen as employing political processes that are morally positive, employing acceptable means to gain beneficial ends (Block 1987; Bolman and Deal 1991; Donnithorne 1992).

Because politics is concerned with power, a chair must quickly learn the sources of power in the department and the interrelationships that enable those sources to be used effectively. Success in this endeavor could be the crucial factor in the conduct of a successful administration. The chair of an academic department is therefore deeply involved in the political and power interplays in the department, and a chair who wishes to employ political skills must acquire the ability to assess the players and to know precisely the situations under which political behavior will exert a significant impact on departmental planning and management (Bacharach and Lawler 1980; Block 1987).

The chair's concern with power and politics is by no means confined to dealing with the behavior of departmental members. An academic department operates within a two-layer political environment. The inside layer is the environment generated by the internal workings of the parent organization. The second, or outer, layer is the general external environment in which the whole organization operates—an environment that is becoming increasingly hostile and has impacts that could impinge directly on the department or be felt indirectly through the parent organization (Cameron and Tschirhart 1992). In terms of the chair's activities, the relationships that exist between the department and its environment are just as important as those that exist within it.

Consideration of the types of power to be found in organizations is useful in the discussion of organizational politics involving the chair. Two general types of power have been identified (Bacharach and Lawler 1980): authority, which must be associated with the chair, and influence, which might not be.

Authority is a right, sanctioned by the organization and assigned to the position. Implied is obedience by subordinates, with the degree of authority *circumscribed by the formal position statement*. Influence is not fixed on an organizational chart, for it is an informal aspect of power that can be exercised by any of the actors in an organization. Influence is derived from a number of factors, including personality, expertise, possession of knowledge, and a capacity to control opportunities for exploitation.

Consideration of Pfeffer's definition of organizational politics in terms of the two types of power indicates that *influence* forms the basis on which political battles must be fought in a department.

> *Influence is derived from a number of factors, including personality, expertise, possession of knowledge, and a capacity to control opportunities for exploitation.*

Sources of Power in the Department
Office power
Office or structural power is power conferred on the chair through capacities arising from the position of the office of chair in the institutional structure. Being appointed or elected to the position of chair carries with it the opportunity to apply coercion or offer rewards, to acquire detailed information about the operation of the institution and its environment, and to manipulate the symbols of academe. The chair might

then use these tools of the position to discharge the major task of resolving differences of opinion and values among the departmental subgroups (Scott 1981).

The position of chair exhibits great differences in the nature of office power attached to it. In some cases, the chair has a great deal of coercive power arising from the nature and structure of the institution's hierarchy. In other cases, the dominant capability conferred might be acquisition and manipulation of knowledge or the ability to control the symbols of academe in the particular department.

Some chairs might find the conscious exercise of office power difficult to reconcile with their personal values and style. Office power, however, is a source of power that carries with it a set of mutual obligations and expectations between faculty and chairs that are major stabilizing factors in the continual battle of contending views that is always part of departmental life.

Personal characteristics
An individual might have a set of personal characteristics that will lead to the assumption of leadership of a subgroup. Possessing these characteristics enables the exercise of "acts of leading," which "constitute a form of artistry and may involve a variety of creative endeavors, including dramatics, design, and orchestration" (Duke 1986, p. 14).

This particular concept of leadership would seem to be appropriate for leaders of subgroups in an academic department with considerable autonomy, ambiguous processes and outcomes, and incessant maneuvering for prestige. Departmental cultures provide a well-constructed backdrop to a powerful play of the acts of leading by those individuals whose personal characteristics provide them with the drive and skills necessary to assume the role. Chairs are expected to have personal power, a power that must be earned by gaining the respect of faculty members and others in the university and beyond (Tucker 1984, p. 9). A successful chair quickly develops an effective strategy to gain the maximum possible personal power.

Expertise
Members of academic departments have many opportunities to acquire and use specialized knowledge about issues and the workings of the institution. Use of this knowledge, when

the time and conditions are favorable, can exert considerable influence on departmental decision making.

Department members can learn information about the institution through many channels: from membership on committees and senate councils and from external authorities, including accrediting teams and professional associations. Chairs are usually in a position to learn this information formally or informally by communicating with the individuals concerned. Investing time in such inquiries has the potential to relieve much of the pressure that can be exerted by faculty expertise.

Opportunity

Opportunity is not associated with the formal structure of an organization set out on an organizational chart. Instead, it is derived from the informal structure, perhaps a separate network of uncharted interrelationships, or from the informal aspect of formally established positions.

Individuals or groups at any level of authority might find themselves in, or insert themselves into, a space in the organization that provides them with a source of knowledge about individuals and events in the institution. Opportunities then become available to exert influence through coercion and possession of knowledge that could disrupt or delay decisions or activities in the department.

Opportunity is a source of power that exists in almost all organizations, but it is particularly potent in an academic department where the outcomes of decisions are ambiguous and opinions and possible directions widely disparate.

Interest Groups and Coalitions

Individual members of a department, other than the chair, could exercise a significant degree of power in their own right, particularly when power is based on expertise and opportunity. Dominant individuals emerge from time to time, but personal power is not often used by an individual acting alone. Instead, individuals often seek to maximize their power by joining or building one or several interest groups and coalitions (Lee and Lawrence 1985).

The existence of a structure of subgroups is not limited to universities and colleges. All organizations, whatever their purpose, have such a structure of one kind or another, but the nature and structure of the subgroups in an academic department are determined by whether or not a mutual recognition develops of a desirable set of outcomes for each of the issues the department faces.

Interest groups might be single-issue groups or might exist on the basis of a common response to a series of issues. Coalitions are groups in which an ideology has been developed and bargains have been struck after intense discussion and consideration. Such arrangements are concerned with more than one issue and are capable of drawing on and using all of the influence-type sources of power (Bess 1988).

Chairs have always had to contend with both types of groups. Interest groups are not difficult to recognize, and their transient nature allows the chair a significant freedom of action in dealing with them through incentives, accommodation, and the application of office-based power. An interest group, however, might be an emergent coalition (Cobb 1986), and the chair must not ignore its existence or the circumstances that brought it into being.

Coalitions might present more difficulties for the chair as agreement among the members has put a set of mutual obligations and expectations in place. A firm basis for tactical planning and action exists that can develop to a level of sophistication that the chair might find troublesome (Davies and Morgan 1982).

The Department as a Political Environment
In addition to loosely coupled political organizations, universities and colleges might also be considered open systems, as they receive input, apply processes, and produce outputs while constantly interacting with external environments.

Many individuals, groups, events, and circumstances are present in the environment, and all of them could affect the department in a way that necessitates a response. Everyone in the department is affected to some degree by environmental factors, but the chair is the key linking the department to the external environment. The task demands that a successful chair develop a detailed environmental map to determine who or what in the external environment can exert pressure on the department, what the nature of this pressure will be, and how it can best be accommodated (Bardach 1978; Hearn and Heydinger 1985).

Inside environment

A chair's work must be profoundly influenced by the internal workings of the parent organization. Departments struggle to increase the degree of influence that they can exert and the level of prestige that can be acquired as they interact with the individuals and groups that can shape the direction of their operation. Trustees, campus executives, academic committees, resource allocation groups, faculty and student organizations, and a host of others must be influenced to make decisions favorable to the department. The chair is thus always involved in political situations that can have a major impact on the department.

A department that has developed a significant capacity to influence other players and groups in the institution's political structure has acquired institutional power (Dozier-Hackman 1985). Maintaining an acceptable level of institutional power is a prime task for the chair. If a chair is not capable of achieving a workable level of institutional power for the department, then alternative routes of political representation for the department and its faculty will rapidly appear. The result will be the generation of a great deal of internal confusion and conflict within the department as faculty struggle to protect their interests in the face of the chair's political failure. Individual situations fuel the formation of subgroups that feel forced to take positions to safeguard the department, and hostility toward the chair because of the political failure inevitably results.

External environment

The department chair is required to represent the department and the academic discipline in the general community outside the institution. Political activity is required in the community and before state and federal governments, depending on the nature and size of the department (Blocker, Bender, and Martorana 1975). The discipline taught and the degree of autonomy that has accrued to the chair based on the department's power in the institution are important determinants of the chair's external political activities.

Community-level politics arises from interactions between the institution and the local community. They are highly variable, depending on the location and characteristics of the institution and the nature of the surrounding community. The chair must become familiar with the functioning of the community as it interacts with the institution as a whole and with the department, its discipline, its operation, and its individual faculty. Each community has its own particular set of reactions, which can range from complete disinterest to fear and anger, but no matter what form the interaction takes, the impact can be of crucial importance to the effective operation of the department, its chair, and its power base.

Communities have political parties, educational authorities, and local governments, all of which can exert powerful pressures on the way an institution and its individual departments operate. In addition, a wide range of pressure groups, including service clubs, unions, professional associations, chambers of commerce, and others, can exercise considerable political clout if an issue falls within their sphere of interest. Community groups do not form to remain silent and often respond with vigor to real or perceived issues that interest them. They often have the capacity to create situations that have a major impact on the institution and directly or indirectly on the department.

Universities are often authorized by state legislation and must operate within a network of other state legislation and controls, regardless of their primary mechanism of funding. Public institutions are much more involved in direct control, coordination, and resource and program interactions with the state, but many other state laws and authorities can also exercise a powerful influence on private universities and colleges.

Much of the political interaction with the state involves institutional officers higher than the chair, but this fact does not exempt the chair from state politics. A detailed understanding of state officers and legislators and the way they work and can be influenced is necessary if a chair is to maintain the department's position of institutional power within the university.

The federal government is deeply involved in the politics of higher education, and there are no signs of its withdrawal. The government will undoubtedly continue to manipulate higher education policy as a means of accomplishing national and international goals and priorities. All sections of the academic community feel the impact of the federal government's decision making, and the chair, who in most cases has little chance of influencing that policy, is often put in the position of having to implement federally mandated policy or dispense federal resources in the department. Faculty members might have little interest in the wider political scene and see such changes as yet another external intrusion and erosion of autonomy.

Selection and Use of Strategies

A chair works in an organization populated by politically active individuals going about their business in various environments that have significant, often very vigorous, and competing components. No matter how strong the chair's vision of what can and should be done, he or she has little chance of achieving it without spending major amounts of time and effort to develop strategies that can make the vision prevail. "An agenda is inert without a strategy to make it happen" (Bolman and Deal 1991, p. 208).

Chairs need to formulate and execute strategies to achieve their goals, using the tools available to them—their authority and their capacity to exert influence in the institution and in its environment. Chairs must set an agenda and become adept at marshaling support for the strategic goals of that agenda. They must understand the political nature and the circumstances of the situation to construct a strategy that will meet the demands of each situation.

The range of strategies available is enormous, and their selection varies according to the chair's timetable, the degree of resistance expected, and the power of the person or group that is the target of the strategy. Like most phenomena associated with human behavior, it is possible to segment the spectrum of possibilities into groups that exhibit similar characteristics: for this discussion, push strategies, pull strategies, persuasion strategies, preventative strategies, and preparatory strategies (Lee and Lawrence 1985, p. 155).

Push strategies

Push strategies subject target individuals to pressure. Often the chair can use the power of the office for this purpose, but other tactics can be used, including withdrawing cooperation, imposing delays or slowdowns, using disaffected faculty, and injecting social activities into the situation. All are strategies that must be employed with caution, as the outcomes, even if the chair wins, can create conflict, disaffection, or even alienation—effects that could be counterproductive so far as the chair is concerned.

Pull strategies

Pull strategies employ incentives. Strategies that motivate
action favorable to the chair's requirements through the use
of rewards are readily available to the chair. Symbolic rewards
like titles, honors, and desired appointments all fall within
the chair's authority to disburse or at least to influence
strongly. The impact of pull strategies depends to a large
extent on the chair's style of leadership. For example, a trans-
actional leader might employ dramatics, design, and orchestration to enhance his or her personal appeal and charisma,
assisting the faculty's empowerment and inspiring personal
commitment, loyalty, and alliances. These outcomes facilitate
considerably the implementation of the chair's ideas and
direction for the department. Transformational and other types
of leaders might use a range of incentives to support their
particular style as they exercise leadership in various situations.

Persuasion strategies

Drama involves actors who present events by using their skills
of communication and projection to involve, arouse, and persuade an audience to believe and behave in the manner the
actors want. Involvement, arousal, and the use of language
are all strategies a chair can use to persuade faculty members
to align themselves with the chair. Skills involving the use
of language to project a sincere, spontaneous, unpremeditated
image and the favorable impressions that can be generated
by dress, gestures, and expressions are not difficult to learn.
Every chair should seriously consider the conscious acquisition of these skills.

Other avenues of persuasion are open to the chair: preparing persuasive papers, lobbying with faculty leaders and
in some cases the media, and garnering support from outside
experts.

Preventative strategies

A politically adept chair has taken control of the department's
agenda and has worked to understand clearly the political
behavior of departmental members. In this context, control
and knowledge are tools that can be used to prevent a situation's becoming an issue. Directly suppressing information
or using blatant procedural methods to circumvent issues is
a dangerous ploy, but the capacity to control who gets to
know what and when can be an important tactical tool for
the chair.

Preparatory strategies

An ill-prepared politician soon becomes an ex-politician, and the same can be said about a department chair. Without a well-thought-through set of strategies to contain or neutralize pockets of resistance to the chair's agenda, a cloud of political stonewalling, protectiveness of one's own turf, and counter-ploys will descend over the department.

A whole range of preparatory strategies is available, some of them very simple, such as meeting locations and seating arrangements that place the chair in a favorable position. Others include managing the agenda, preparing position papers, and presenting options, all of which can be used to guide discussion along lines acceptable to the chair.

A chair might use any or all of these strategies to bring a matter to resolution. Clearly, successful chairs must have developed skills that will support the use of these strategies, and while natural agenda setters, orators, communicators, negotiators, persuaders, and visionaries have always existed, they do not necessarily become chairs of academic departments.

Skills for Implementing Strategy

Situations and individual differences among chairs prevent the development of a comprehensive inventory of skills. Chairs cannot, however, avoid being political strategists, and they must be equipped with skills that enable them to execute their strategies. Although chairs might bring to bear a vast array of skills, they should seriously explore four basic areas: (1) impression management, (2) agenda setting, (3) networking and support gathering, and (4) negotiation and bargaining. These areas are not mutually exclusive; in fact, they overlap considerably, and impression management in particular pervades all four areas.

Impression management

Chairs work in situations where they are subject to a great deal of evaluation. If they are to survive and prosper under this constant scrutiny, they must have some means of managing the identities that superiors, faculty, and staff assign to them. Social situations are created by the identities of the people present, and the ensuing interactions tend to be controlled by the nature of those identities (Tedeschi and Melburg 1984).

Not surprisingly, then, most people attempt to control their image in the presence of others (Baumeister 1982; Goffman 1959). Such behavior is a way of obtaining desired reactions from others, among them perhaps acceptance, friendship, perceived competency, and other characteristics that can create a favorable impression of the person's identity. This behavior is impression management.

In turn, impression management depends largely on self-presentation, which can be described as the conscious or unconscious attempt to control self-reliant images before real or imagined audiences (Schlenker 1980). Proficiency in self-presentation is a necessary skill for chairs, for it enables construction of a perceived identity that will permit control of their interactions with others in the organization. Sometimes these skills are intuitive, but often they are not.

Many strategies for self-presentation are available to chairs; four of the most general and common are the perception of competence, ingratiation, exemplification, and intimidation (Leary 1988).

Competence is the basis of expert power, and the perceptions that faculty form of a chair's competence largely affect their judgment as to whether or not the chair is an appropriate leader.

Ingratiation is concerned with influencing faculty members' liking for the chair. It can be facilitated by presenting a friendly, warm, and accepting image. Desired outcomes of ingratiation are enhanced loyalty and more positive relations within the department. It is unfortunate that the word has acquired a somewhat negative connotation through popular usage, but it describes an essential social process that is one of the glues of society.

Exemplification is the projection of an image of dedication, discipline, and selflessness. This trait enables chairs to be seen as exemplars for the department and creates the impression that the chair has the right to perform the often onerous task of sitting in judgment of the work of others in the department.

Intimidation is possibly the most difficult self-presentation of all. The projection of credible threats without resorting to the raw power of the office is not a simple accomplishment.

It must be emphasized that these skills are not techniques of deception. For example, an attempt to impress as an exemplar without exemplary achievements is a useless subterfuge. But to fail to include legitimate exemplary characteristics into the identity assigned to the chair is a waste of an important capability of leadership.

Agenda setting

A chair without a firmly held and very clear set of goals should not have accepted the position of chair. Such goals are the visionary part of the agenda, a set of strategies to implement the vision the other part (Kotter 1988).

The first and most important set of skills is concerned with determining which forces are for and which are against the agenda—listening, gathering opinions, patience, and persistence. After listening, identifying key players, searching for the basis of their opinions, and gaining a feel for the source and strength of likely resistance, the chair can construct an agenda that retains the essential vision. The chair must be prepared to accept compromise and to accommodate conflict with the department's goals so that the agenda can be seen as workable in terms of available resources.

In essence, the skills needed are careful listening, assessment, and compromise without abandoning the vision.

Networking and support gathering

Creating a support network simply means finding out who can help and how supporting relationships can be built. The fundamentals of the processes involved are interpersonal, and the chair deliberately sets out to gain support from others by playing on their ideas, emotions, and aspirations to gain their interest, confidence, and support (Kanter 1983). Such work involves bargaining, creating obligations, making alliances, manipulating expectancies, conferring prestige, and so on. The chair needs to focus energy on the individuals or groups involved using means such as luncheons, meetings, telephone calls, office visits, or social occasions as media through which ideas are sold, bargains struck, rewards promised, and support solicited—all in terms of the opinions and ideas of the target to be networked.

In universities and colleges, the internal network targets for the chair include departmental opinion leaders and groups, committee members, senates, centers or institutes, councils, regents, trustees, senior executives, and advisers. Outside targets include legislators, coordinating commissions, professional associations, foundations, and accrediting agencies.

A chair without a firmly held and very clear set of goals should not have accepted the position of chair.

Negotiation and bargaining

An extensive literature on negotiation and its practice in essence is based on negotiation as a process that is used when the parties involved have some interests in common and other interests in conflict. Every chair must understand the process of negotiation, because conflict is an inherent characteristic of higher education institutions and because many others in the institution can be expected to have very-well-developed skills of negotiation.

An often recommended approach to negotiation is the Win-Win Method (Fisher and Ury 1981), which involves what can be termed "principled bargaining" built around four action statements:

- Separate people from the problem (do not attempt to defeat the other parties).
- Focus on interests, not positions (look for the factors underlying positions).
- Invent options for mutual gain (look for possibilities that might bring gain to both sides).
- Insist on objective criteria (standards of fairness of both substance and procedure).

The skills of a successful negotiator have often been studied. Some basic principles have emerged, but it is clear that the need for particular skills in negotiating and bargaining are highly situational. At certain times some skills are vital; other times they are irrelevant (Kniveton 1989). Generally, the skills studied have been concerned with face-to-face contact, but this element is only one in the process of negotiation, as the absence of effective strategies will always negate good negotiation. Even if the strategies are good and fair, they will have little chance of success if the parties relate unfavorably to each other.

A negotiator must acquire certain skills: (1) be endlessly patient; (2) be a good enough listener to instill in others the confidence that they are being heard and understood; (3) be persuasive; (4) be able to assess the real wants and aspirations, and be able to resist other parties; (5) be able to build good interpersonal relationships with the other parties; (6) be aware of his or her own capacities and limitations; and (7) be not easily moved from a position but able to accept compromise if necessary. Negotiators must know what they want, know what the other parties want, and know how to move toward what all parties want.

It is not possible to create a no-fail recipe for the structure and conduct of negotiations. One very broad framework, however, includes five stages: (1) preparation, (2) discussion, (3) proposal, (4) bargaining, and (5) close (Lee and Lawrence 1985, p. 171).

Certainly, information about what is wanted and how it will be achieved is the essential first step of any process of negotiation. All relevant information must be collected, analyzed, and organized to underpin the strategies that will be used. The other stages will be activated at some point during negotiation, but their nature and format will depend largely on the characteristics of the situation.

A better approach than describing stages might be for the chair to enter negotiations with a series of targets in mind (Kniveton 1989). The aims would be to establish and clearly define the other party's position and demands, to assess the other party's targets or hoped-for achievements, and to determine the points of resistance (the levels of concession or compromise beyond which the other party will not go).

When these parameters are established, the process of striking a bargain is greatly simplified, and effective resolution of conflicts becomes a real possibility.

Summary

Chairs work in complex organizations that to a large extent are open political systems. Departmental decision making is deeply involved with the maneuvering between groups and coalitions to maximize autonomy and control.

The chair has two environments to address: the internal university environment and the external environment in which political forces arising from the local, state, and federal governments all affect the department and its decision making.

A successful chair understands the workings of political processes and is skilled in their use. Political practice is not generally thought of as a good means of achieving desired ends, but it can be. A "principled" chair striving to achieve a beneficial vision for the clients of higher education uses political processes for beneficial reasons and is not uncomfortable doing so.

A politically skilled chair must acquire a high degree of competence in the strategies and tactics of impression management, agenda setting, networking, and negotiation. Together, these skills can provide a set of tools that the chair can use to build and maintain a successful department.

THE ROLE OF THE CHAIR IN FACULTY EVALUATION AND DEVELOPMENT

Evaluation, the process of judging performance, is one of the most powerful opportunities for development available to a department chair, and "probably no other activity has more potential for strengthening or weakening a department over a period of years" (Tucker 1984, p. 216). Although evaluation creates anxiety for both the chair and the faculty member, it provides the platform for in-depth communication and the occasion to shape the direction of the department and the priorities of the faculty member.

This section examines the purpose of evaluation, fundamental questions to be asked for a successful evaluation, and present and emerging instruments and activities to implement evaluation. Through orientation, mentoring relationships, interventions in teaching and research, and the process of helping faculty refocus their efforts, evaluation can provide a critical and natural bridge for the chair to facilitate faculty growth and development.

The Purpose of Evaluation

For a chair to be effective in evaluating faculty, the reasons for the evaluation and the techniques employed need to be clear to both the chair and the faculty member. Evaluation can provide:

- A focus in an ambiguous environment with often unclear expectations for work;
- Direction and reinforcement for individual faculty members;
- An opportunity to reinforce the mission, priorities, and use of departmental resources;
- Explicit expectations so that faculty are freed to channel their energies and faculty colleagues can clarify how they can be helpful to each other;
- Occasion to define with the individual the needed professional development opportunities to support the department and the activities needed for continued growth; and
- Opportunity for assessing performance.

While evaluation can be perceived as a high-risk situation, chairs must also realize it has the potential for a high payoff. One of its clearest benefits is preventing low performers from decreasing departmental morale. Identifying expectations for professional development is also crucial.

What does it take for a fair, credible evaluation? The literature on faculty evaluation provides widespread consensus on what is required. For evaluation to be a systematic, fair, and accepted process, participants must agree that evaluation is a fundamental component of the department. Everyone involved must understand and accept that evaluation is necessary and that real benefits can be achieved if the purpose is clear. The question should not be whether evaluation will occur but what will happen and how (Miller 1979; Seldin and Associates 1990; Tucker 1984).

Issues Affecting Evaluation

At least four questions should be answered to develop a consensus about the process to be used and to build an effective system:

- What is to be measured?
- How is it to be measured?
- Who is to measure it?
- What are the quality indicators or criteria?

Answers to these questions will be affected by the nature of the institution, the mission of the department, and the interests of faculty members. A detailed response to each question provides the framework for understanding the involvement and role of the department chair.

What is to be measured?

Whatever is measured should be congruent and consistent with institutional, departmental, and faculty expectations. Differences in the expectations of those involved must be clarified and negotiated. Typically, the focus in evaluation is on research, service, and teaching; however, the emphasis on these categories is influenced by the nature of the institution (liberal arts, comprehensive, or research, for example), present or changing departmental expectations, and the talents and interests of individual faculty.

In discussions of what is to be measured, all aspects of departmental and faculty activities should be examined, reducing the possibility of ignoring individual contributions. Some aspects of the evaluation will, however, be emphasized so important personnel decisions can be made. The decisions or recommendations that chairs make about promotion, tenure, merit pay, special graduate standing, contract renewal, and annual or semiannual performance are based on evaluation (Creswell 1985). Evaluation will also provide valuable information on overall professional progress and areas that need improvement or further development.

How is it to be measured?

Once a department or academic unit has decided what is to be evaluated, then involved parties must decide the "how" of evaluation. If the parties decide that teaching is an important activity to evaluate, then what to measure must be considered.

Self-evaluation. Faculty have historically provided some information through informal and sometimes formal self-evaluation. Although the individual's own evaluation is not sufficient, comprehensive, or entirely objective, the faculty member is an important source to consider. Aspects of the individual evaluation that can be particularly helpful include outcomes that cannot or are not easily measured by other means (e.g., extracurricular activities, interactions with other programs or colleagues). Individuals can also describe the less visible professional development they have accomplished. If departments are to use information from self-evaluation, however, then the criteria and the form needed must be clarified and agreed to. A number of self-evaluation forms, particularly for formative evaluation, are available in the literature (see, e.g., Braskamp, Brandenburg, and Ory 1984; Weimer, Kerns, and Parrett 1988).

Student ratings. During the 1960s, a dramatic movement occurred in the United States to use student ratings to assess teaching. Many institutions mandated the use of such ratings for personnel matters, and an immense amount of research and analysis indicates student ratings can be valid and reliable sources to measure some aspects of teaching (Cashin 1989; Miller 1987; Seldin 1980).

Students have demonstrated that they can make valid and reliable judgments about the delivery of instruction, the assessment of instruction, and the instructors' availability to students. Although a few evaluation centers have developed valid and reliable instruments to measure these aspects of teaching, individual institutions have used various evaluation consultants to perfect their own instruments. Whatever instrument is used, it must be valid and reliable to ensure credibility and consistency.

Peer ratings. Research on teaching indicates that faculty colleagues can make useful judgments about some aspects, including mastery of subject matter, curriculum development, course design, and administrative details (Cashin 1989; Seldin 1992). Although peer ratings, particularly classroom visitations, have received considerable attention in the last few years, they still are not frequent (Seldin 1991). While such visits could be appropriate to generate additional data on mastery of subject matter and course design, they should not be the only way to gather information about a teacher's effectiveness.

The use of multiple sources of data in teaching evaluations must be clear to both the chair and the faculty member. Different data sources should be used to assess particular aspects. A promising development is the concept of the teaching portfolio. Long used by artists and architects, the portfolio provides a means to describe and assess teaching in the context in which it takes place, with particular emphasis on outcomes and processes that could lose their special flavor in more generalized teaching assessments (see Edgerton, Hutchins, and Quinlan 1991; Millis 1991; and Seldin 1991 for suggestions about developing a portfolio and examples where they are being used). Documentation in the portfolio could be one response to the complaint that promotion and tenure committees know less about one's teaching ability than about his or her research (Seldin 1991, p. ix, citing McKeachie 1986).

A portfolio enables faculty to document and display their teaching in the particular context where it occurred (Edgerton, Hutchins, and Quinlan 1991, p. 3). The portfolio "is to teaching what lists of publications, grants, and honors are to research and scholarship" (Seldin 1991, p. 3).

Five steps can be used to create a portfolio (Seldin 1991): (1) summarize teaching responsibilities, (2) select criteria for effective teaching, (3) arrange the criteria in order, (4) assemble the supporting data, and (5) incorporate the portfolio into the curriculum vitae. A framework for defining and documenting seven dimensions of teaching (what you teach, how you teach, change over time, rigor of academic standards, student impressions, developmental effects, and collegial assessments) produces the appropriate information for a portfolio (Urbach 1992).

Because portfolios are a new development, proponents of their use do not have any documented evidence of their effectiveness. Some advantages of the portfolio, however, appear to be that it offers an individualized picture of a professor's teaching, a qualitative and quantitative presentation of teaching, and a composite description based on multiple sources; provides a powerful tool for improvement (Edgerton, Hutchins, and Quinlan 1991); analyzes the connections to the contexts and personal histories that characterize teaching, making it possible to document the unfolding of both teaching and learning over time (Edgerton, Hutchins, and Quinlan 1991; Shulman 1989); and prompts more reflective practice and improvement (Edgerton, Hutchins, and Quinlan 1991).

Portfolios also have certain disadvantages (without clear documentation at this point): most promotion and tenure committees do not have experience in evaluating portfolios; the portfolio requires a greater commitment of time to examine the complete record; and administrators and promotion and tenure committees could have more difficulty making qualitative judgments, as teaching history is presented in context rather than in comparison.

The preparation of portfolios improves when faculty attend instructional workshops and work with other faculty to prepare them (Seldin, Hutchins, and Millis 1992). Training for promotion and tenure committees and administrators in how to evaluate portfolios is also necessary. Important questions should be addressed in assessing portfolios: Is real evidence of accomplishment present? Is the faculty member's reflective statement consistent with the syllabus and outcomes? Is the faculty member improving? Are outcomes of learning documented? Another major question to be resolved is the appropriate peer group for review, and the answer can vary depending on institutional type.

Certainly the use of portfolios provides an opportunity to experiment (pilot projects by senior, well-respected faculty are possible) and to forge a balance between quantitative and qualitative aspects of work. Individual colleges and campuses as well as national groups advocate teaching as a form of scholarship that should encourage research on the use and effectiveness of portfolios.

Research and service should also be examined to determine what is to be measured. An examination or assessment of productivity in research might include quantitative and qualitative measures, peer judgments, and measures of eminence (editorships, honors, invited papers) (Creswell 1985; Miller 1987). A matrix and a process for determining weight or value of professional service contributions are useful to assess applied research, consultation and technical assistance, instruction, products, and clinical work or performance (Elman and Smock 1985). Such a matrix would provide a system for documentation and for determining who should evaluate, the criteria to be used, and the weighting factor.

Who is to measure it?

Once it has been decided what to measure and how to measure it, the next decision for the chair and the department is who will measure it. The purpose for collecting the data could determine the people who will measure it. For example, if the information is to be used for professional development, then the faculty member might want to collect and maintain control of the data.

If the faculty member has a service appointment, discussion should focus on who is appropriate to measure this function. For example, if the faculty member has an off-campus program with a specific clientele, the clientele and the faculty member should design a process to determine whether practices or behavior has changed. Faculty colleagues again could make some judgments about the faculty member's knowledge and the quality of the program, particularly as it compares to other programs.

What are the quality indicators?

In any area to be evaluated, faculty should reach an agreement about quantity and quality indicators; otherwise, judgments can be the object of undue disagreement.

For example, publications can be counted in the examination of a faculty member's research performance. Many times, quantity is what is reported in describing a faculty member's contributions or achievements. Yet some judgment must also be reached about the quality of the publications. One of the most frequent procedures is to assess the publication's place in the hierarchy of publications in the discipline, that is, from the most elite to the least prestigious.

Depending on the assignment, however, some faculty might not conduct research that would be appropriate for the most elite journals. Chairs need to consider some alternative ways of determining scholarly contributions appropriate for faculty contributions.

Under the concept of "scholarship reconsidered" (Boyer 1990), a faculty member who focuses on application of knowledge should be evaluated in terms of how well the concepts and knowledge are applied in the field. The individual involved and the department could define what the indicators would be of quality work in application. If a faculty member were to focus on research on teaching in his or her academic field, then publication would be expected in teaching journals, both inside and outside the discipline. The goal would be to assess whether this work contributes to greater understanding of teaching and has significance in teaching others outside the classroom.

An examination or assessment of productivity in research might include quantitative and qualitative measures, peer judgments, and measures of eminence.

Evaluation Systems

The current press is toward systems that evaluate all areas of faculty performance. Such schemes should reflect the expectations of the department. (For a discussion of the options in such a system, see Tucker 1984, pp. 143–74.) The levels of complexity can be described as assignment of points for each area of activity (Tucker [1984] suggested a scale of 0 to 4, in which 0 represents unsatisfactory and 4 excellent), assignment of points based on the percentage of assignment to a particular function, and assignment of points based on a weighting for departmental priorities.

Within these systems, departmental members must define what each rating represents and what criteria are to be used for each level. Only then can what the ratings represent and the department's priorities be clear (Braskamp, Brandenburg, and Ory 1984; Tucker 1984).

The Relationship of Evaluation and Faculty Development

The literature on evaluation and faculty development contains frequent comments that care should be taken to separate the two functions. A key question separating the functions is, "What is the information to be used for?" *Summative data* are most often used for personnel decisions, or *evaluation.*

Distilling information into summative units is similar to what is done in reducing a mound of data to a grade in a student's classroom record.

On the other hand, *formative information* is used for improvement or *development.* The process is most frequently described in instructional situations in which midterm assessments are made and shared with the instructor to improve course instruction. The information collected is treated as confidential and strictly under the control of the faculty member. If any of the information is to be shared, it would be at the faculty member's discretion. Outside of communicating the faculty member's commitment to professional improvement, however, much of the formative data would not be particularly helpful in making personnel decisions. For decisions about promotion and tenure, four or five "global" questions might be appropriate (see Seldin 1991); 25 to 30 diagnostic questions to address improvement would also be needed. Instruments like IDEA (Instructional Development and Effectiveness Assessment [Miller 1987]) and TABS (Teaching Analysis by Students [Clinic to Improve 1974]) provide information that can be used for both purposes.

The process of evaluation can undoubtedly provide some keys to faculty members' needs and highlight areas that require improvement, such as skills, knowledge, or motivation.

The Chair as Faculty Developer

Chairs have always performed some role in faculty development. The earliest forms identified were encouragement and support of attendance at professional meetings and participation in sabbatical programs. Over the past decade, chairs have been encouraged to play a larger and more personal role in faculty development. Beginning a decade age (Tucker 1984), chairs were provided a list of responsibilities for faculty development and activities they could suggest to faculty to pursue professional development (see also Menges and Mathis 1988). A study focusing on the strategies excellent chairs used to facilitate faculty growth and development identified the kinds of faculty development issues chairs were addressing and the strategies they used to resolve issues or problems (Creswell et al. 1990). Chairs in that study suggested that:

- Faculty development is a responsibility shared by the individual faculty member, the chair, and in some cases the department.
- Chairs are motivated by various reasons to take on the responsibility of faculty development. Although little evidence indicates that it is part of the job description, chairs say they took on the responsibility because they "cherish one's colleagues," "it's part of the job," or "if they don't do it, then who will!"
- Through efforts to open communication about dreams, goals, activities, achievements, and shortcomings, chairs help to prevent the faculty's disengagement and isolation.

Chairs in this study identified several issues as crucial in facilitating the growth and development of faculty:

- *Getting faculty started:* Chairs should consider how they can address the needs of new faculty.
- *Teaching:* Chairs can take an active role in promoting the teaching agenda and enhancing individual teaching.
- *Research:* Chairs can provide a sense of direction and emphasis for research and help faculty through mentoring and other activities.
- *Refocusing or redirecting faculty:* Chairs have the opportunity to facilitate the growth of faculty by being open to and encouraging new directions more in line with faculty and departmental needs.
- *Personal concerns:* Several strategies are available to help chairs help faculty resolve personal concerns (Creswell et al. 1990; see also Boice 1991a, 1991b, 1992; McKeachie 1986; and Sorcinelli and Austin 1992 for identification and resolution of these issues).

Getting faculty started
A great deal of literature in the last five years has focused on getting faculty started. With the high cost associated with hiring and the difficulty in finding replacements, it seems like a good investment to ensure that faculty get started properly. Additionally, it sends a message that the institution cares.

Many of the activities associated with getting started have focused on informal and formal orientation sessions, on mentoring, and on addressing specific needs of new or junior faculty. Orientation sessions are not new, particularly formal college or university sessions in which faculty are acquainted with available resources. Perhaps more unusual are regular meetings of chairs or deans and faculty to address a number of philosophical and specific issues about research, teaching, service, and the conduct of departmental business (see, in particular, Boice 1992; Jarvis 1991; and Sorcinelli and Austin 1992).

Mentoring extends the notion of continued orientation through personal and professional relationships. In its most basic form, mentoring is a senior person's helping a junior faculty member understand how things get done and providing the emotional support to address the many situations that a new person must overcome or resolve. Some literature suggests that mentoring leads to an increase in academic production (Boice 1991a; Kroger-Hill, Bahniuk, and Dobos 1989), but few systematic studies of these relationships are available.

The word "mentoring" has often been broadened or used in new ways in the literature. Some suggest that "communication support behaviors" might be a better term to address other kinds of facilitative relationships (Kroger-Hill, Bahniuk, and Dobos 1989) rather than stretching the classic definition of mentoring. New minority faculty could be particularly at risk, and interventions, including encouragement of mentoring relationships, might be helpful (Boice 1991b, 1992).

Teaching or instruction
Teaching is a crucial function that involves most faculty, and chairs have identified issues involving teaching for both beginning and established faculty. Particularly for new faculty, chairs have identified concerns about organization, level of difficulty for students, and the amount of time committed to teaching at the expense of other activities, and some suggested solutions for improvement include fewer classes, including released time from one course the first year (Fink 1984), in-depth discussions with the chair or colleagues (Creswell et al. 1990), mentoring relationships (Boice 1991a, 1991b, 1992; Sorcinelli and Austin 1992), and classroom visitations (Lucas 1989).

Many chairs are concerned about competency in the subject matter, an inadequate commitment to teaching, and inability to relate to students for faculty in their departments. Some chairs might choose to intervene to a great extent, including visits in the classroom and meeting with the faculty member, but the academic norms of tenure and academic freedom often inhibit such powerful interventions.

In times of high tuition, institutional accountability, and possible shortages of faculty, teaching will continue to receive attention. Particularly for tenured faculty, a number of campuswide and individual strategies can help improve teaching (Seldin and Associates 1990). The Fund for the Improvement of Post Secondary Education, for example, has provided financial support for a number of projects that address creating an environment encouraging and rewarding teaching.

Many chairs have used teaching improvement centers to help faculty address concerns about teaching. More chairs are involved with individuals, however, to improve teaching (see Lucas 1989, 1990 for particular strategies). Efforts range from modeling effective teaching to direct departmental action (departmental meetings focused on teaching) and classroom interventions (observations in the classroom and videotaped classes with feedback).

Research and writing

Chairs continuously identify research as an issue for professional development. Because institutions of higher education have the responsibility to enhance existing knowledge and to create new possibilities through abstraction and reflection, this issue is not unexpected. In institutions with a strong focus on research, most faculty appear to support this expectation. What is more surprising is the expectation for research that has arisen in some comprehensive and liberal arts institutions (Bowen and Schuster 1986), although those that do are transitional, attempting to change the institution's focus by providing more graduate courses and research grants (Creswell et al. 1990). Many of the traditional faculty hired to be teachers were unsettled, and even bitter, about this transition.

Several studies in the last five years have investigated how to facilitate productive research. The professional socialization process and a successful pattern of publication are major factors in the commitment to research and its continuing productivity (Creswell 1985), but much literature does not provide concrete suggestions for how to encourage faculty who are less productive.

Several research-based strategies indicate success in encouraging more writing and research (Boice 1990). Time management/contingency planning indicates that by structuring short but designated time periods, faculty can increase their writing and incorporate it as part of their weekly routine. Another process deals with disillusioned midcareer faculty, in which "field workers" (chairs or faculty) can be trained to reengage faculty and increase productivity (Boice 1992). Both programs use specific strategies and have proven payoffs, something chairs are continuously attempting to find. Three primary roles of chairs have been identified that address increasing faculty's productivity in research: administrative (providing resources and allocating time for scholarly work), advocacy (promoting and publicizing faculty who improve performance), and interpersonal (mentoring, collaborating, encouraging, and challenging faculty) (Creswell and Brown 1992).

Refocusing or redirecting faculty

Many chairs can identify faculty members who do not seem to be moving professionally—those who are "stuck" (Kanter 1981), "plateaued" (Bardwick 1986), or "snoozing."* The question is how to move these faculty forward in their careers. Evaluation could be the event that precipitates addressing the need to make changes. Many chairs recognize that adults often change interests and have different needs over time and so must adjust or refocus their interests. The chair can open discussion, shift assignments, and plan for professional development (Creswell et al. 1990).

One activity that has shown promise is to provide career consulting or counseling for faculty (see, e.g., Wheeler 1990). In many ways, career consulting is parallel to instructional consulting, with a focus on an individual faculty member's career. This service provides a means for faculty to clarify and to examine new directions, both internal and external to the institution.

A number of campuses have attempted to address structures or programs to help midcareer faculty refocus or redirect their efforts. At the University of Nebraska–Lincoln's Institute of Agriculture and Natural Resources, for example, faculty can voluntarily enter a program that provides a two-and-one-half-day planning institute and a planning process to move in new directions (Lunde and Hartung 1990). A recent longitudinal study of 10 faculty who participated in the program between

---

* W.J. McKeachie 1982, personal communication.

1983 and 1986 indicates that they not only make external changes (teaching methods and use of technologies, interpersonal skills and new roles), but that they also develop a new attitude toward making changes. A midcareer professor commented, "[It] gave me a perspective I never had before: Don't get too comfortable in a situation and don't be afraid to change . . ." (Lunde et al. 1991, p. 132).

These programs reduce the faculty's isolation and disengagement. Those who take the journey not only change themselves, but also challenge others to move on from plateaus. More programs of this nature and more research and evaluation (short term and long term) of the process and the results are needed; it is simply good risk management.

Personal concerns

Faculty members' personal problems can interfere with their work. A study of department chairs identified five personal issues: relationships with students, staff, and faculty, difficulty associated with dual careers, exclusion and alienation in the department, health, and personal disorganization (Creswell et al. 1990). An additional area often identified is faculty who are chemically dependent, often estimated to be 6 to 10 percent of faculty (Scanlon 1986; Thoreson and Hosakawa 1984).

Although chairs often express concerns about being in the role of psychologist and usually have limited, if any, training in assessing personal problems, they are often expected to make preliminary judgments about the seriousness of these issues and problems. They can determine whether the problem is short term or long term. A problem with alcoholism, for example, is a long-term situation that requires systematic intervention, often with the cooperation of family, peers, and counselors, while a faculty member who has suffered a personal loss might require only short-term support (perhaps an attentive listener and temporary help with responsibilities).

Overall, chairs can be helpful to faculty by listening and helping to clarify options. Particularly in more serious situations and in situations where they feel less capable, they can refer faculty to counseling services inside or outside the institution. A number of universities have employee assistance programs, and most institutions have some type of psychological services available (for a more complete treatment of strategies to address personal issues and problems, see Creswell et al. 1990, pp. 94–103).

THE INFLUENCE OF INSTITUTIONAL TYPE AND ACADEMIC DISCIPLINE ON THE CHAIR

How the department chair functions and the leadership strategies he or she uses are influenced by the type of institution, the leadership approach of the institution, and the academic discipline, all of which have implications for the selection, training, and development of chairs.

Types of Institutions

The multitudinous colleges and universities in the United States represent a great variety of roles and missions. The most recent and complete classification of American colleges and universities (Carnegie 1987) lists more than 3,500 institutions according to their academic purpose and size, in 10 different categories.[3] While diversity in institutions—"one of the ideological pillars of American higher education" (Birnbaum 1983, p. 37)—is one of the system's great strengths, such diversity makes it difficult to generalize about the roles, tasks, and duties of department chairs and other educational leaders. The Carnegie classifications, based on funding, programs, and size, offer little help in identifying how the various institutions actually function.

---

3. The categories include *Research Universities I,* which offer a full range of baccalaureate programs, receive at least $33.5 million in federal research and development (R&D) funds annually, and award at least 50 Ph.D.s each year; *Research Universities II,* which offer a full range of baccalaureate programs, receive between $12.5 million and $33.5 million in federal R&D funds annually, and award at least 50 Ph.D.s each year; *Doctorate-granting Universities I,* which offer a full range of baccalaureate programs and award at least 40 Ph.D.s each year across five or more academic disciplines; *Doctorate-granting Universities II,* which offer a full range of baccalaureate programs and award at least 20 Ph.D.s each year in at least one discipline, or 10 or more Ph.D.s across three or more disciplines; *Comprehensive Universities and Colleges I,* which enroll at least 2,500 full-time students and offer baccalaureate programs and, with few exceptions, graduate education through the master's degree, with more than half of the baccalaureate degrees awarded in two or more occupational or professional disciplines; *Comprehensive Universities and Colleges II,* which enroll between 1,500 and 2,500 full-time students and offer at least half their baccalaureate degrees in two or more occupational or professional disciplines, and might also offer graduate education through the master's degree; *Liberal Arts Colleges I,* which are highly selective institutions, primarily undergraduate, and award at least half of their baccalaureate degrees in arts and sciences; *Liberal Arts Colleges II,* which are primarily undergraduate institutions and award more than half their degrees in the liberal arts; *Two-year Colleges and Institutes,* which offer certificate or degree programs through Associate of Arts; and *Professional Schools* and other specialized institutions, which offer a full range of degrees with at least 50 percent in a single, specialized field.

Other typologies of universities and colleges, however, can be more helpful in analyzing organization and describing style of management. One proposal includes three models of university governance: bureaucratic, collegial, and political (Baldridge 1971a). The bureaucratic model was derived from the work of Weber (1947), who characterized a bureaucracy as a network of social groups dedicated to limited goals and organized for maximum efficiency, as hierarchical and tied together by formal chains of command and systems of communication.

The collegial model of higher education organization and governance, on the other hand, is based on the notion of a "community of scholars." It emphasizes the professional authority of the faculty and a prescriptive notion about the operation of the educational process. Some predict its demise on the basis of growing bureaucratization, collective bargaining, state control, and centralization (Baldridge et al. 1978).

The "invisible tapestry" of organizational culture is an appropriate metaphor with which to begin an analysis of the different types of institutions (Kuh and Whitt 1988; Tierney 1988), as educational institutions are made up of informal and formal structures. But neither the bureaucratic nor the collegial model adequately describes the reality of the modern university (Baldridge 1971a), leading to the premise of the political model (Baldridge 1971b). The political model emphasizes the making and unmaking of allegiances, the normative role of conflict, the existence of interest groups in a pluralistic culture, and the role of negotiation, bargaining, and influence.

The political model has been further developed into a model of the university as an "organized anarchy" (Cohen and March 1986), for it shows a lack of coordination and control. Allocation of resources, for example, is based on whatever process emerges out of competing priorities, and decision making in such an institution is produced by the system "but intended by no one and decisively controlled by no one" (p. 34).

A distinguishing feature of educational organizations is that they are "loosely coupled" systems (Weick 1978). While events in the organization respond to each other, the various parts continue to preserve their own identity and separateness. And although some educational institutions as systems are obviously more loosely coupled than others, such coupling is a feature of them all, especially because educational organizations espouse ambiguous goals (Baldridge et al. 1978).

At the same time, institutions of higher education have significant elements, especially in their administrative structure, where coupling might need to be constantly tight (Weick 1978). It is difficult to imagine, for instance, a loosely coupled payroll system. Similarly, changing degrees of looseness or tightness could become necessary as a result of environmental changes. Increasing government involvement in higher education, for example, is likely to lead to a need for greater accountability and hence for tighter coupling.

In addition to the bureaucratic, collegial, political, and organized anarchy models is a fifth model, the cybernetic institution (Bensimon, Neumann, and Birnbaum 1989; Birnbaum 1988), drawn from the notion of the self-correcting or cybernetic entity (Ashby 1956). Birnbaum (1988) further applied the concept of coupled systems to all five models and identified patterns of loose and tight coupling in each institutional type, finding, for example, that institutions that could be characterized as bureaucratic had more evidence of tightly coupled systems than did institutions that more closely matched the political or anarchical models. While an institution of higher education is unlikely to be perfectly described by any one of the five models or by one coupling system, such analysis is nonetheless useful.

The Chair in Different Types of Institutions

Symbolic acts and unobtrusive management are important within a system of organized anarchy (Birnbaum 1988), and the cybernetic model of higher education management emphasizes the importance of recognizing the elements of all four earlier models in each institution (Bensimon, Neumann, and Birnbaum 1989). Negative feedback loops provide continuous opportunities for corrective action, and leaders change their behavior according to changing situations. "Thus, effective leaders are those who can simultaneously attend to the structural, human, political, and symbolic needs of the organization, while ineffective leaders are those who focus their attention on a single aspect of an organization's functioning" (Bensimon, Neumann, and Birnbaum 1989, p. 65).

The next step is to move from these attempts to classify higher education institutions as models of operation and style

Negative feedback loops provide continuous opportunities for corrective action, and leaders change their behavior according to changing situations.

to an understanding of how institutional differences affect campus and departmental leadership. A random sample of 334 four-year institutions was used to develop case studies of seven different kinds of higher education institutions (Chaffee and Tierney 1988). The researchers identified distinctive patterns of organization, culture, decision making, and leadership in each model and found internal and external pressures for change that could modify an institution's traditional values and style. Institutions could change so much that they move from one organizational model to another (Baldridge 1971a).

The organizational structure of departments is intimately connected with the university's size, the administrative complexity of the general campus, and the institution's prestige (Murray 1964). A study of 185 four-year schools and 64 community colleges found that governance and management vary systematically in different types of institutions (Baldridge et al. 1978), and the authors suggested a classification system that combines the features of the Carnegie list based on programs and size with those of the organizational and cultural models. They thus proposed eight types of institutions: Private Multiversities, Public Multiversities, Elite Liberal Arts Colleges, Public Comprehensives, Public Colleges, Liberal Arts Colleges, Community Colleges, and Private Junior Colleges. These eight types vary consistently in three basic organizational characteristics: environmental relations, professional task, and size and complexity. In particular, the farther one moves from Community Colleges to Public Colleges to Elite Liberal Arts Colleges to Multiversities, the more influential are the faculty, the less administrators dominate, the less environmental influence affects the institution's autonomy, and the less influential is the union. Further, larger and more prestigious institutions are characterized by a high degree of faculty expertise and by strong academic departments (Baldridge et al. 1978). Such institutions give their department chairs a greater level of autonomy than other schools and more discretion in selecting faculty, controlling courses, and making decisions about promotion and tenure. In most institutions, however, budgets are centrally controlled.

Private, less selective liberal arts colleges and community colleges exhibit a high level of bureaucratic control (Bensimon, Neumann, and Birnbaum 1989). Rational skills, such as producing results and defining problems and solutions, are rated higher in such institutions than collegial skills like motivating others and being a team member. Management style in collegial institutions, on the other hand, stresses consensus, shared power, and participation. The notion of an elected head, a "first among equals," is dominant. The group's norms and values are the guide by which an elected chair might operate in such an institution, with a strong emphasis on consultation (Bensimon, Neumann, and Birnbaum 1989). Those in positions of leadership in politically oriented institutions can be considered mediators or negotiators between shifting power blocs (Bensimon, Neumann, and Birnbaum 1989). Their power is based on control of information and manipulation of expertise rather than on an official position or the respect of colleagues.

Much of the literature dealing with leadership and management in higher education according to institutional type has focused on the role of the president. But it is not difficult to see how the various styles, constraints, and opportunities afforded by particular models are also applied to department or division leaders. Chairs in community colleges, for example, are categorized as "a sort of vicar of the dean" (Underwood 1972, p. 156). The chief tasks for a chair are handing down decisions, giving orders, and generally keeping the faculty in line.

In a large, public university, the chair is an agent of faculty consensus (Mahoney 1972). The ideal chair in a state college has good character, an understanding and appreciation of the role of administration, the appropriate job and people skills, and outstanding professional ability (Heimler 1972). A department chair in a major research university saw the task as "running something that is more like a symphony orchestra than a competitive team" (Burgan 1986, p. 3). "Fighting off pirates" and "scrabbling for money" are growing in importance in the chair's work, and chairs often now have to take an active role in cultivating donors. Departments in liberal arts colleges are protective of their turf, fighting for resources and students (Wolverton 1990). On the other hand, chairs in professional schools preside over departments that share common goals and objectives.

Different types of institutions place different demands on their chairs (Creswell et al. 1990). In a research university, it is the norm for a chair to return to a teaching and research position after three to five years, and so an individual must

remain professionally active and current in the discipline during the period he or she is chair of the department. According to one earth sciences chair in a doctorate-granting school, "A chairmanship can ruin a research career" (Creswell et al. 1990, p. 16). In other types of institutions, however, chairs could be less subject to such pressures, especially if they see their careers as developing toward a full-time administrative position.

Chairs in baccalaureate institutions are likely to regard themselves as faculty rather than administrators (Tucker 1984). Such chairs share disciplinary knowledge and allegiance with their peers and are usually able to achieve consensus on matters involving curriculum and departmental policy. The chairs of community college divisions, however, often find such consensus difficult. With faculty members from diverse backgrounds, such chairs are less prone to a collegial style of management and are more likely to work closely with central administration than chairs in four-year institutions. Further, chairs in community colleges rank the importance of administrative and bureaucratic tasks much higher than their university colleagues, who place greater emphasis on activities that are faculty related (Tucker 1984).

Just as important, however, is the additional finding that chairs from community colleges and universities agree substantially about the major tasks of a chair (Tucker 1984). Both groups include the following five responsibilities in the top 10, though not necessarily in the same order:

- Fostering good teaching,
- Maintaining faculty morale,
- Recruiting and selecting faculty,
- Communicating needs to the dean and interacting with upper- level administration, and
- Updating curriculum courses and programs (p. 31).

A total of 54 tasks and duties confront almost all chairs (Tucker 1984), related to the 28 possible roles that chairs can play.

A survey of 5,830 faculty in 65 universities and colleges across the country from all major types of institutions asked faculty to rate a total of 458 department chairs in terms of their leadership and quality of performance on 15 typical responsibilities (Knight and Holen 1985). The researchers used the Departmental Evaluation of Chairperson Activities for Development (DECAD) system developed by Kansas State University, which involves two forms: one that asks faculty to rate the performance of chairs on 15 responsibilities and a second that asks for faculty perceptions of the chair's leadership on items identical to the Leadership Behavior Description Questionnaire (LBDQ) developed at Ohio State University. More specifically, the LBDQ-type items explore the chair's task orientation ("initiating structure") and relationship orientation ("consideration") (Halpin 1966). For all 15 responsibilities, across departments varying greatly in size, type of institution, and control, those chairs rated high on both "initiating structure" and "consideration" received the highest performance ratings. Thus, training for chairs should emphasize a high level of skill in both tasks and relationships, and professional development programs for chairs should assist in improving the behaviors strongly associated with these styles of leadership.

Training and Developing Chairs in Different Institutional Types

Perhaps the most striking theme in the literature concerning the roles and tasks of department chairs in different types of institutions is the common recognition of the need for greater preparation and training for chairs (Bennett 1988; Knight and Holen 1985; Monson 1972; Tucker 1984). Eighty-two percent of the 39 department chairs in one study had no training or orientation for the job (Bragg 1981), and perhaps all chairs "begin with an absence of training" (Goldberg 1990, p. 17). Another survey of 200 chairs in 70 universities found considerable concern over the task of learning how to be a chair (Creswell et al. 1990). Few institutions seem to have a formal process for such induction.

In one survey, chairs in a large state community college system were dissatisfied with the in-service training for their positions (Curtis 1990). Perhaps the acquisition of skills by new chairs should be emphasized less and programs designed to develop high levels of structure and consideration emphasized more (Knight and Holen 1985). A survey of faculty and chairs in a statewide community college system and in a large West Coast university concluded that all chairs need "skills that foster friendly cooperation among faculty" (Groner 1978, p. 141).

If a core set of responsibilities is common to chairs across the full range of institutional types, then training and development programs for chairs should reflect both core attributes and conditions specific to institutions. Chairs in small and specialized institutions need especially to understand how the budget structure has been developed and what assumptions have been used (Falender 1983). Chairs of large departments need organizational and communication skills quite different from those needed in small departments (McKeachie 1976). A survey of deans of arts and sciences in 350 universities with more than 10,000 students, for example, found that management of and responsibility for the budget were the hallmarks of a successful chair (Moxley and Olson 1988). Not many new chairs would likely have these skills.

Departmental Typologies

The view of institutional organization and mission substantially affects the task and role of the department chair. Does the discipline of a department, however, have a similar impact? A consideration of typologies of departments is useful before attempting to answer this question.

A typical large, modern university might house 75 different academic disciplines, each in its own department (Anderson 1976). These disciplines are responsible for the primary tasks of the university: the advancement and enhancement of knowledge and the transmission of what is already known. A discipline is thus both a method and a body of knowledge. How is it possible to generalize about the variety implicit in this structure of 75 potentially different methods and bodies of knowledge?

One response is a three-dimensional clustering of academic departments (Biglan 1973a), with departments located on each of three continuums:

- *Hard or soft,* with hard departments characterized by a paradigm or agreed-upon set of problems and methods and soft departments having no clearly delineated paradigm.
- *Pure or applied,* with pure departments not particularly concerned with the practical applications of their work.
- *Life or nonlife system,* with life system departments emphasizing the study of living systems and nonlife system departments lacking an emphasis on organic objects.

Thus, all departments fall into one of eight categories:

Hard, nonlife, pure (e.g., math or physics);
Hard, nonlife, applied (e.g., civil engineering);
Hard, life, pure (e.g., botany or physiology);
Hard, life, applied (e.g., horticulture);
Soft, nonlife, pure (e.g., English or history);
Soft, nonlife, applied (e.g., management or law);
Soft, life, pure (e.g., anthropology or psychology); and
Soft, life, applied (e.g., education) (Biglan 1973a).

Chairs of departments classified in this way vary widely in their level of involvement with colleagues, their preference for and time spent on teaching, research, and service, and their scholarly productivity (Biglan 1973b). A review of related studies shows differences among discipline orientations on a wide array of student and faculty characteristics (Creswell and Roskens 1981). The three-dimensional model of departments (Biglan 1973a) and the various studies emanating from it (e.g., Biglan 1973b; Creswell, Seagren, and Henry 1980; Neumann and Boris 1978; Seagren et al. 1986; Smart and Elton 1976) remain valuable guides for alerting chairs to the likely emphases and requirements of their work.

Impacts of Discipline on the Role of the Chair

An application of Biglan's departmental model to 1,646 chairs in 32 public doctorate-granting institutions (Smart and Elton 1976) identified four major role areas for chairs: faculty, coordinator, researcher, and instructor. Significantly, chairs in hard departments spent relatively more time on their role as researcher (obtaining and managing grants and contracts; recruiting, selecting, and supervising graduate students) than their colleagues in soft departments.

Further, chairs of soft departments spent more time in their instructional role (teaching and advising students) than did their colleagues in hard departments (Smart and Elton 1976), supporting the finding (Biglan 1973b) that faculty in soft departments expressed a greater preference for and spent more time on teaching than faculty in hard departments. Chairs of pure departments spent relatively more time on their faculty role (planning professional development of faculty, maintaining morale, and reducing conflicts) than their colleagues in applied departments and less time on their role as coordinator, and chairs of life system departments devoted relatively more time to their role as researcher than chairs from the nonlife system departments (Smart and Elton 1976).

Perhaps a major cause of these differences among department chairs, related to the departmental differences among faculty, is the chair's previous experience as a graduate student and as a faculty member within a discipline (Smart and Elton 1976). While professional development programs for chairs should have a broad focus because of the diverse and complex nature of the tasks facing all chairs, such programs should also recognize the distinctive demands and roles that exist in different types of departments. Programs could be of most value if they include specialized training in those responsibilities where chairs spend a disproportionate amount of time. Chairs of hard departments, for instance, might be helped by enhancing their skills as researchers, while chairs of soft departments would be likely to benefit from additional development of their instructional abilities (Smart and Elton 1976).

A contrary perspective is that those chairs who lack particular skills could well benefit from acquiring them. Thus, it would be appropriate to offer to all chairs, of both hard and soft departments, access to specialized developmental activities to maximize opportunities for departmental leadership. A survey of 120 chairs in a large midwestern university and four state colleges, testing Biglan's model in relation to chairs' perception of their own developmental needs, showed that chairs in the hard departments expressed the strongest need for training in assessing relationships among departmental personnel (Creswell, Seagren, and Henry 1980). Chairs from the social sciences, on the other hand, perceived greater need for development in soliciting external research grants. The needs for such training could well indicate skills not obtained during graduate education or disciplinary socialization.

Elements of Biglan's model were extended to faculty perceptions of chairs' leadership in 80 academic departments, both hard and soft (Neumann and Boris 1978). Effective hard-discipline departments developed one-factor (task-oriented) leadership only. Effective departments in soft disciplines, on the other hand, developed two-factor (task-oriented and people-oriented) leadership. Departments with low effectiveness adopted an opposite style of leadership for both hard and soft departments. Thus, it is necessary to develop different styles of leadership for chairs in different discipline areas and at different stages of the department's development. Differences in discipline might provide a context for the administrative development of chairs (Booth 1982).

A study of factors important for faculty development and departmental vitality stresses the way in which chairs from a variety of disciplines emphasize communication, acquisition of resources, and motivation to enhance productivity (Seagren et al. 1986).

Academic Discipline and Training for Chairs

A number of organizations and institutions are now involved in providing developmental activities for new and continuing chairs (Bennett 1988; Creswell et al. 1990; Jennerich 1981), among them the American Council on Education, the Kellogg Foundation within the State University System of Florida, and the International Institute for Academic Leadership Development established by the Center for the Study of Higher and Postsecondary Education at the University of Nebraska and the National Community College Chair Academy of Maricopa Community College (Seagren and Filan 1992). Some associations and professional groups also offer regular developmental activities for chairs in their academic area.

Department chairs are often confronted by the need to shift away from discipline or departmental loyalty to embrace a loyalty to the wider institution (Bennett 1988). Much of the role conflict that chairs experience stems from such a shift. Nonetheless, a small, often fugitive, literature concerns the chairing of departments from the perspective of particular disciplines, much of it in the form of conference papers or in disciplinary journals and newsletters. Though the literature is often anecdotal, impressionistic, and autobiographical (Moxley and Olson 1988), it points to a need for more systematic research into how chairs from different disciplines perceive the challenges of their position.

Some professional organizations have already accepted responsibility for a number of these issues. For instance, the Association of Departments of English (ADE) has conducted summer institutes for new English department chairs (Jennerich 1981). Publications sponsored by the Modern Language Association of America and the *ADE Bulletin* include articles dealing with issues of concern to English and other language chairs (Burgan 1986; Millichap 1986). Gatherings of groups like the Conference on College Composition and Communication have also produced reflective papers on issues of specific concern to English chairs, such as the chair's role in facilitating relationships between literature and writing faculty (Milne 1988) and the need for English chairs to receive in-service training in budget preparation and financial management (Moxley and Olson 1988). A survey of 150 English chairs in universities with enrollments between 5,000 and 12,000 (Shreeve, Brucker, and Martin 1987) reveals a frequent need for additional administrative and counseling skills.

Other disciplines, including theater (Whitmore 1988), psychology (Kimble 1974, 1979), and engineering (Magana and Neibel 1980), have also organized workshops for chairs or have produced material to guide them. Generally, these activities have focused on issues of concern to all chairs, including budgets, faculty development, hiring, and promoting, but have had some emphasis on matters of concern to a particular discipline (see, e.g., Kimble 1974 on the need for psychology chairs to develop skills required for chairing a large and growing department and Magana and Neibel 1980 on the dangers of becoming caught up in too much administration). Highly developed skills of delegation are necessary if chairs are not to lose touch with their research and their links to industry.

Summary

Types of institutions, the differences among types in the orientation of faculty, the running of day-to-day business, and approaches to leadership are distinct and widely discussed in the literature. Less well known is how these differences shape the orientation and behaviors of chairs. The trend—and it requires extensive empirical support—is that community colleges and some four-year schools operate with a framework of chairs in an administrative role with strong powers in the bureaucracy of the organization. In small liberal arts colleges and the most prestigious universities, chairs operate more as a team member or a colleague and often serve as chair temporarily or for a specified period of time. Thus, the most distinct differences by type of school might be reflected on a continuum from a team, faculty-oriented model of leadership to a more bureaucratic approach of an "administrator."

These differences are seen most clearly in efforts to train and develop chairs in different institutional settings. To relate affiliation with a discipline to chairing presents an even greater challenge. Given the differences in time spent on roles and tasks, authors call for a sensitivity to differing roles and tasks in training and staff development for chairs. This sensitivity could be most apparent in professional organizations that have developed workshops and training seminars for chairs from their own disciplines. An examination of the literature of these professional organizations and a review of their professional meeting programs suggest that topics for chairs address timely issues, such as budgets, faculty development and evaluation, hiring and promotion, staff, and the impact of size on the functioning and operation of the department.

FUTURE CHALLENGES FOR THE CHAIR

Given the ambiguity of the chair's role and the relatively high turnover of chairs in many departments, clarifying the expectations of the position and commitment to continued development of chairs should be emphasized to a greater extent. Readers are encouraged to consider their needs and to use the various materials to make a "do list" for continued improvement. A basic agreement or job description can be clarified through the use of a checklist of roles and tasks that can form the basis for exchange with faculty and upper-level administration. Beyond the focus on the present chair's responsibilities and continuing development, it is proposed that chairs promote the development of their successors and department leadership in anticipation of the department's future needs.

Many chairs complain that with lack of clarity and little orientation, they learn by trial and error or even trial by fire.

Chairs occupy an ambiguous role because they are neither fish nor fowl and as a result of the variation in responsibilities across institutional types. Seldom is the role circumscribed through a job description or other document. Many chairs complain that with lack of clarity and little orientation, they learn by trial and error or even trial by fire. As a result, turnover among chairs has increased (Carroll 1990; Creswell et al. 1990), with the average tenure about five years. Under these circumstances, chairs should be provided the means or tools to define their work so as to facilitate their effectiveness.

An Effective Agreement

Increasing public scrutiny and calls for accountability have placed more emphasis on departmental leadership. New ways to forge agreements on roles and responsibilities are needed, as new demands are being made on chairs with limited training for the position and, with considerable turnover, fewer chairs with experience are available. A checklist of roles and responsibilities synthesizing the literature (see Appendix A) helps administrators and chairs to clarify roles and tasks (see, e.g., Creswell, Seagren, and Henry 1980; Creswell et al. 1990; Dressel, Johnson, and Marcus 1971; Heimler 1972; McLaughlin, Montgomery, and Malpass 1975; Norton 1980; Smart and Elton 1976; Tucker 1984).

The following procedures are suggested in the use of the checklist in Appendix A:

- *Independently work through the list.* Mark areas of responsibility or nonresponsibility. Indicate the extent of your responsibility regardless of how you marked the first category. And then determine your level of competence in each task or responsibility by indicating the professional development needed.

- *Determine who should be involved in clarifying roles and responsibilities.* Although this requirement could vary by institution, your immediate supervisor and faculty or faculty representation are crucial.
- *Exchange the checklist and discuss* commonalities and differences.
- *Develop an agreement* emphasizing major roles, specific responsibilities, means of resolving differences, and professional development needed to address responsibilities.
- *Finalize an agreement* clarifying those involved.

Certainly responsibilities will vary, not only because of differences in the expectations of individual chairs but also because of the nature of the institution and the size of the department. In a large department in a research-oriented institution, for example, the chair might not be expected to teach classes or to participate directly in academic affairs. In a small department or division of a small liberal arts college, on the other hand, the chair might have major responsibilities for instruction and few direct responsibilities as a chair. Profiles of chairs often differ, and no one set of responsibilities is right for all situations. Those included in the determination of an agreement might also differ.

Leadership Frame(s) Needed
Presidents and other upper-level administrators are expected to provide institutional leadership, including symbolic and transformational leadership (Bennis and Nanus 1985; Bensimon, Neumann, and Birnbaum 1989; Burns 1978; Cameron and Ulrich 1986). The same expectation needs to be encouraged from chairs.

Leaders can use four frames or "lenses" to reframe organizations:

- *Human resource frame,* emphasizing new skills, opportunities for involvement, and providing support. (See Creswell et al. 1990 for a more complete picture of this frame, with many strategies and activities of chairs to empower faculty.)

- *Structural frame,* emphasizing clarity of roles and relationships. Structural considerations are central to a chair's responsibilities and are a common focus in organizations.
- *Political frame,* focusing on creation of arenas so issues can be negotiated.
- *Symbolic frame,* emphasizing interpretation and reinterpretation of events (Bolman and Deal 1991).

Given the changing environment of higher education, chairs should develop the flexibility to use all four frames. Overindulgence in or dependence on any one frame can lead to the chair's ineffectiveness. For example, the symbolic frame requires the ability to move to a new level of understanding through the use of metaphors, new interpretations, and events that symbolize change. Without reframing, events will consistently be interpreted to keep the status quo. For example, if a department desires to be at the forefront of its field, the image might be of creating the wave rather than riding or finding the wave. The symbolism is focused on the creative process as the priority rather than the nuts and bolts of implementation.

Changing the frame of reference for a department is not simple. Awareness of the different frames, observation of others effective in their use, and practice in using them with feedback about effectiveness can all be helpful in bringing about change. Chairs can also use other faculty in their unit with talent in the use of any of these frames to encourage departmental change.

Chairs often show an understanding of structural and political frames, possibly because of their experience and observations in institutions, but they might need to become more familiar with a human resource frame and a symbolic frame (see, e.g., Creswell et al. 1990 illuminating the chair's role in facilitating the faculty's growth and development). With an aging faculty and many new faculty, chairs will face a more bipolar faculty (Schuster, Wheeler, and Associates 1990), requiring constant attention to creating new opportunities and providing the structure and support for faculty to be successful. Use of such programs as sabbaticals, leave without pay, and professional development leaves will help faculty move to meet the demands. (See Menges and Mathis 1988 for a useful list of strategies to encourage and support faculty, and Boice 1992; Jarvis 1991; and Sorcinelli and Austin 1992 for strategies to develop new faculty. These resources provide suggestions for orientation to the institution, support mechanisms, and strategies for development of faculty in teaching, research, and service roles.)

Issues Chairs Must Address
Key issues that will face chairs and require leadership during the 1990s and beyond can be seen as contributing to the goal of enhanced departmental and institutional prestige through individual professional empowerment. Chairs need to discuss the issues with faculty and to devise appropriate strategies for dealing with them. A key focus needs to be on the way in which the department's response will lead to the strengthening of its members and of its disciplinary and organizational standing.

The current decade has already produced new pressures and opportunities. Education is being called upon to address and solve national problems. Chairs are now required to lead their department's response to major issues and changes occurring across higher education (Bennett 1988):

- *Quality control.* The strengthening of academic standards is a major concern in the face of allegations concerning the declining value of a college degree and the need to ensure that students receive the education they deserve at a reasonable cost. Some higher education institutions have used Total Quality Management and Continuous Quality Improvement (Sherr and Teeter 1991) because of this concern.
- *Diversity and gender.* Many more women are now completing graduate school and will significantly change the face of higher education employment, including positions of leadership (Waerdt 1990).
- *Funding.* Alternative sources of funding must be developed as the relative proportion of public support for higher education continues to decline. Community colleges and research universities will find increasing competition for funds. Certainly for the remainder of the 1990s, chairs will have to address finding alternative funds and reallocating resources. Chairs will need to play active roles in fundraising and institutional development (Bregman and Moffett 1991; Layzell and Lyddon 1990; Summers 1991).

- *Faculty recruitment and retention.* The 1990s and the early years of the 21st century will see many faculty retire, creating a major opportunity for chairs to hire and develop outstanding new faculty. Because of declining numbers of graduate students in the 1980s and 1990s, many observers predict a seller's market. Chairs will need to develop a competitive edge to attract and retain the faculty they want and need to maintain quality (Hynes 1990).
- *Professional development.* Calls for greater accountability and demonstrated efficiency will grow, placing substantial pressure on all chairs to indicate how their faculty are equipped to deal with new knowledge and concerns. Chairs themselves will need to undertake developmental activities in administrative and other tasks (Sorcinelli and Austin 1992).
- *Faculty workload.* Increasing scrutiny of the outcomes of higher education, especially by state coordinating authorities and state legislatures, will lead to greater calls for firm guidelines for faculty workloads and professional commitments. Chairs will need to play a leadership role in developing appropriate means of devising and monitoring these guidelines (Boyer 1990; Yuker 1984).
- *Evaluation.* Competition for vacant positions and public pressure will heighten the need for effective and continuing faculty evaluation. Regular post-tenure evaluation will facilitate professional development, requiring chairs to engage in career planning with faculty (Creswell et al. 1990; Licata 1986; Seldin 1984).
- *Minority students and faculty.* The opportunity for much more minority participation in all programs and in competition for faculty positions will require complex and sensitive leadership. Minority administrators (including chairs) will be in a special position to assist in these processes (Green 1989).
- *Ethics.* A pressing need exists to ensure that institutions of higher education have come to grips with the daily implications of their ethical principles and that faculty and students are aware of them. Chairs are responsible for ensuring that ethical considerations are part of the normal deliberative processes in their area (Cahn 1990; May 1990). Issues of academic freedom and accountability and shifting priorities for faculty have important ethical

implications. Chairs engaging in collective bargaining are encouraged to understand fully any dimension of a bargaining agreement that affects their roles and responsibilities.

Professional and Departmental Development

Chairs must be active in identifying and addressing their own professional development. Too often the daily press of activities takes precedence, and personal and professional development is deferred. Chairs should build an agenda to continue to grow and develop just as they encourage their faculty to develop. Chairs might want to consider the following areas in their plan.

Identify and upgrade skills

Consistently in the literature, chairs cite the need to improve their negotiation and conflict-resolution skills (Bennett 1983; Tucker 1984). In changing times, these skills become even more crucial. But other skills are necessary as well: evaluation, communication, long-range planning, public relations, political maneuvering. Fortunately, chairs have many means available for their development (see Green and McDade 1991):

- *Mentors.* Chairs can often gain perspective and guidance from on-campus and off-campus mentors, perhaps more experienced chairs or upper-level administrators.
- *Reading materials.* A number of substantive newsletters are now available, and an increasing number of books and articles focus on chairing.
- *Workshops/seminars.* A range of activities is provided nationally by the American Council on Education, the Institute for Academic Leadership Development, and regional and on-campus programs.
- *Tests and self-assessment instruments.* Many leadership-style assessments are available for development. The Departmental Evaluation of Chairperson Activities for Development instrument from Kansas State University provides a good baseline for chairs.
- *Conferences.* National conferences, such as the Kansas State Chair Conference and National Community College Chair Conference, and individual disciplinary societies provide chair-oriented activities associated with a national or special meeting.

- *Learning groups.* On a number of campuses, chairs have formed groups that provide some learning experiences and continuing development activities.
- *Work projects.* Often work experiences can be tailored to encourage professional development through projects or new tasks.
- *Networking.* Exchanging information, ideas, perspectives, and resources is crucial to success. Evaluations of conferences often indicate that networking was of greatest value, and chairs frequently rank their discussions and exchanges as the highlight of conferences and workshops.

Develop learning processes

Reflective practice (Argyris and Schon 1978; Schon 1983) and systems thinking (Senge 1991) provide means of analysis to clarify and learn from difficult problems. These learning processes require constant practice, but they can be most helpful. They often lead to learning in groups in which feedback can be provided and reflective analysis accomplished.

Use of these learning processes can lead to major conceptual and behavioral breakthroughs. For example, chairs, through reflective practice in tackling a problem that did not come to a satisfactory solution, might be able to see that their actions did not fit their espoused theory of action. With a commitment to analysis, theory and practice can become congruent (see Senge 1991).

Design a professional development plan

Chairs can design a professional development plan to address their needs, perhaps using the worksheet in Appendix B. Chairs can address any number of areas in their professional development, including:

- *Routine* areas that occur repeatedly, such as scheduling, budgeting, registration, and correspondence.
- *Problem-solving* areas that require either a long- or short-term solution, with the emphasis on a solution for the present as well as for the longer term.
- *Innovative or developmental* areas that require redesigning, such as a redesigned curriculum, new programs, or new degrees.
- *Professional growth,* which might include planning, conflict management, evaluation, and budgeting.

- *Community service,* which might include town/gown relations or the role of the institution in the community. The plan might include providing economic development training or support for community agencies.
- *Institutional priorities or institutionwide directives,* which might include retaining students, excellence in teaching, and more and bigger grants.*

Chairs can use these categories as a format for designing their professional development plan and might also want to incorporate institution- or discipline-specific categories. Whatever format is used, however, chairs should engage peers and upper-level administrators in developing, supporting, and implementing the plan.

The Future of the Department
Perhaps the most important responsibility for the department chair is included in fostering departmental leadership. Four areas are important to the future of the department.

Create, develop, and maintain departmental data bases
For a unit or department to continue to be understandable and its leadership assumable by others, departmental data bases, structures of governance, and decision-making procedures should be well defined and documented. More than just shuffling papers, chairing involves a commitment to build the necessary structures and processes to keep the unit functioning effectively and efficiently and to provide evidence for identifying the need for change and for evaluation.

Mentor others as leaders
The chair is central in encouraging the development of leadership through assignments and the creation of opportunities. The chair not only develops the leadership ability of all faculty but also promotes the possibilities for formal leadership—including chairs of the future. In some instances, a faculty member might be designated the next chair and released at least part time to apprentice for the position, becoming involved in scheduling, budgeting, and other departmental functions. Institutions should support these efforts to increase

---

*C. Bland 1989, personal communication.

efficiency, promote excellence, and avoid the trauma often associated with change in leadership.

Prepare for one's own demise
Chairs need to think and plan for their exit from the position so that they will leave at an appropriate time in their professional and personal lives (Kimble 1979). Too often, chairs allow circumstances—including pressures to stay because no new leader is available or because the change would be departmentally or organizationally inconvenient—to influence their decision about when to step down as chair. Such situations are not in the long-term interest of the chair, the department, or the institution.

Encourage ongoing vision and planning for the department
The literature on departments and chairs contains little discussion of long-term visions for departments. Departmental leadership cannot afford to be short-sighted, however. Discussions about the current and future stages and needs of the department ensure the projection and development of needed leadership. To achieve the department's stability and continuity of leadership requires a serious commitment and understanding that planning is more than hiring good people and maintaining the usual routines.

Recommendations to Improve the Chair's Effectiveness
The following recommendations for chairs, higher-level administrators, researchers, and policy makers can improve the selection, training, and practice of chairs. The recommendations for faculty can make those tasks easier for the first four groups.

Chairs
- *Gain a clear understanding of your role and tasks in accepting or continuing in the position of chair.* Update your roles and responsibilities if you are already in the position. Given the variety of institutional types, individual talents, and units' needs, negotiate priorities and agreements, using the suggested checklist of roles and responsibilities to aid in clarification.
- *Make time to develop a professional development plan for yourself.* Simply learning on the job is not enough.

In some instances, a faculty member might be designated the next chair and released at least part time to apprentice for the position. . . .

Include mentoring, peer learning, and targeted workshops and seminars in your planning.

- *Keep your own career plans well in mind.* Whether you intend to return to your faculty position or move to another administrative position, set some time frames to examine your progress and level of satisfaction. Maintain control of your career with long-range planning and do not succumb to pressures from others.

Higher-level administrators (vice chancellors and deans)

- *Expect and encourage chairs to negotiate agreements on roles and responsibilities and to set out scenarios for their careers* (five years as chair, then back to the faculty, on to another administrative position, or a new decision about whether to continue an administrative career).
- *Expect and encourage chairs to prepare and follow a professional development plan that addresses concerns and future directions.* Develop a process for providing personal and financial support as well as suggesting activities to accomplish the plan. Provide mentoring if appropriate and desired.
- *Expect and encourage the unit or department to incorporate long-term planning that considers future needs and emerging leadership.* This planning should be considered just as important as which faculty are selected, what courses are taught, or how much financial aid for research is sought.

Researchers

- *Study departments and chairs in longitudinal situations to clarify and encourage departmental planning and leadership development over extended periods of time.*
- *Examine the process of how chairs negotiate agreements about their roles and responsibilities,* seeking to identify differences in institutional patterns. Examine expectations across varying stages of the department.
- *Study styles of leadership, skills, and frames of reference of chairs in departments making successful changes.* Chairs who use all of the organizational frames, including the human resource and symbolic frames, would be expected to be more successful.

Policy makers

- *Place a greater priority on chairs as academic and symbolic leaders to be able to help departments meet continuing changes.*
- *Understand the complex nature of chairing a department and that no one model will meet all the needs. Encourage experimentation.*
- *Reward or encourage the rewarding of outstanding performance by chairs.*

Faculty

- *Recognize and encourage long-range planning and leadership development in the department.* Do not allow continued leadership by expediency rather than thoughtful and continuous planning.
- *Commit to continued professional development for all higher education personnel, including your chair.* This development must be more than disciplinary work and should include planning, communication, and activities that make a well-rounded professional.

Summary

Given the ambiguity of the chair's role and the high turnover among chairs, chairs need to negotiate agreements on roles and responsibilities to clarify expectations for them. Chairs need to use all four frames—human, structural, political and symbolic—in providing leadership for the department. Chairs must recognize the issues they will face in the 1990s: quality, diversity and gender, faculty recruitment and retention, professional development, faculty workload, evaluation, minority students, the faculty and ethics, for example. Chairs should develop a plan for their own development and clarify present and future needs of the department.

ROLES AND RESPONSIBILITIES OF THE CHAIR: A Checklist

Area of Responsibility	Responsibility				Extent Responsible								Professional Development
	Is Responsible		Should Be Responsible		Very Little		Some		Considerable		Very Great		N | S | C
	R	NR	R	NR									
Faculty													
• Recruit and select faculty					1	2	3	4	5	6	7	8	
• Prepare and conduct orientation programs					1	2	3	4	5	6	7	8	
• Assign faculty responsibilities					1	2	3	4	5	6	7	8	
• Encourage development of each faculty member					1	2	3	4	5	6	7	8	
• Stimulate faculty research and publications					1	2	3	4	5	6	7	8	
• Evaluate faculty performance					1	2	3	4	5	6	7	8	
• Provide feedback to faculty					1	2	3	4	5	6	7	8	
• Administer merit and salary					1	2	3	4	5	6	7		
Staff													
• Hire staff					1	2	3	4	5	6	7	8	
• Orient staff					1	2	3	4	5	6	7	8	
• Evaluate staff					1	2	3	4	5	6	7	8	
Students													
• Recruit students					1	2	3	4	5	6	7	8	
• Help students register					1	2	3	4	5	6	7	8	
• Advise and counsel students					1	2	3	4	5	6	7	8	

N = No need
S = Some need
C = Critical need

ROLES AND RESPONSIBILITIES OF THE CHAIR: A Checklist (cont'd.)

Area of Responsibility	Responsibility				Extent Responsible								Professional Development			
	Is Responsible		Should Be Responsible		Very Little		Some		Considerable		Very Great			N	I	S	I	C
	R	NR	R	NR												
Academic Affairs																
• Prepare for accreditation or program reviews					1	2	3	4	5	6	7	8				
• Update curriculum/courses					1	2	3	4	5	6	7	8				
• Foster good teaching in unit					1	2	3	4	5	6	7	8				
• Promote affirmative action					1	2	3	4	5	6	7	8				
• Prepare enrollment projections					1	2	3	4	5	6	7	8				
External Affairs																
• Develop relationships with business and community groups					1	2	3	4	5	6	7	8				
• Seek external funding					1	2	3	4	5	6	7	8				
• Represent department to the public					1	2	3	4	5	6	7	8				
Finance and Facilities																
• Prepare budget					1	2	3	4	5	6	7	8				
• Allocate dollars to priority activities					1	2	3	4	5	6	7	8				
• Monitor budget					1	2	3	4	5	6	7	8				
• Manage facilities and equipment					1	2	3	4	5	6	7	8				

N = No need
S = Some need
C = Critical need

ROLES AND RESPONSIBILITIES OF THE CHAIR: A Checklist (cont'd.)

Area of Responsibility	Responsibility				Extent Responsible								Professional Development
	Is Responsible		Should Be Responsible		Very Little		Some		Considerable		Very Great		N I S I C
	R	NR	R	NR									
Departmental Functions													
• Build and maintain databases					1	2	3	4	5	6	7	8	
• Develop long-range plans					1	2	3	4	5	6	7	8	
• Create a positive work environment					1	2	3	4	5	6	7	8	
• Communicate needs to upper administration					1	2	3	4	5	6	7	8	
• Conduct unit meetings					1	2	3	4	5	6	7	8	
• Create unit committees					1	2	3	4	5	6	7	8	
• Schedule classes					1	2	3	4	5	6	7	8	
• Process paperwork and answer correspondence					1	2	3	4	5	6	7	8	

N = No need
S = Some need
C = Critical need

PROFESSIONAL DEVELOPMENT WORKSHEET

Name _____

Objectives (What will I do?)	Method of Assessment (How will anyone know I did it?)	Expected Achievement (What is the value of it?)
1.		
2.		
3.		
4.		
5.		
6.		

Signed: _____   Date: _____

Agreed to: _____

Source: State University System of Minnesota.

REFERENCES

The Educational Resources Information Center (ERIC) Clearinghouse
on Higher Education abstracts and indexes the current literature on
higher education for inclusion in ERIC's data base and announce-
ment in ERIC's monthly bibliographic journal, *Resources in Education* (RIE). Most of these publications are available through the
ERIC Document Reproduction Service (EDRS). For publications cited
in this bibliography that are available from EDRS, ordering number
and price code are included. Readers who wish to order a publication should write to the ERIC Document Reproduction Service,
7420 Fullerton Rd., Suite 110, Springfield, VA 22153-2852. (Phone
orders with VISA or MasterCard are taken at 800-443-ERIC or
703-440-1400.) When ordering, please specify the document (ED)
number. Documents are available as noted in microfiche (MF) and
paper copy (PC). If you have the price code ready when you call
EDRS, an exact price can be quoted. The last page of the latest issue
of *Resources in Education* also has the current cost, listed by code.

Anderson, G.L. 1976. "Organizational Diversity." In *Examining
Departmental Management,* edited by J.C. Smart and J.R. Montgomery. New Directions for Institutional Research No. 2. San Francisco: Jossey-Bass.

Argyris, C., and D. Schon. 1978. *Organizational Learning: A Theory
of Action Perspective.* Reading, Mass.: Addison-Wesley.

Ashby, W.R. 1956. *An Introduction to Cybernetics.* London: Chapman
& Hall.

Bacharach, S.B., and E.J. Lawler. 1980. *Power and Politics in Organizations.* San Francisco: Jossey-Bass.

Baldridge, J.V. 1971a. *Academic Governance: Research on Institutional Politics and Decision Making.* Berkeley, Calif.: McCutchan.

———. 1971b. *Power and Conflict in the University: Research in
the Sociology of Complex Organizations.* New York: John Wiley
& Sons.

Baldridge, J.V., D.V. Curtis, G. Ecker, and G.L. Riley. 1978. *Policy Making and Effective Leadership: A National Study in Academic Management.* San Francisco: Jossey-Bass.

Bardach, E. 1978. *The Implementation Game.* Cambridge, Mass.: MIT
Press.

Bardwick, B. 1986. *The Career Plateau.* New York: American Management Association.

Baumeister, R.F. 1982. "A Self-Presentational View of Social Phenomena." *Psychological Bulletin* 91: 3–26.

Bennett, J.B. 1982. "Ambiguity and Abrupt Transitions in the Department Chairperson's Role." *Educational Record* 63(4): 53–56.

———. 1983. *Managing the Academic Department.* New York: ACE/
Macmillan.

———. 1988. "Department Chairs: Leadership in the Trenches." In
Leaders for a New Era: Strategies for Higher Education, edited

by M.F. Green. New York: ACE/Macmillan.

Bennett, J.B., and D.J. Figuli, eds. 1990. *Enhancing Departmental Leadership: The Roles of the Chairperson.* New York: ACE/Macmillan.

Bennis, W.G., and B. Nanus. 1985. *Leaders: The Strategies for Taking Charge.* New York: Harper & Row.

Bensimon, E.M., A. Neumann, and R. Birnbaum. 1989. *Making Sense of Administrative Leadership: The "L" Word in Higher Education.* ASHE-ERIC Higher Education Report No. 1. Washington, D.C.: George Washington Univ., School of Education and Human Development. ED 316 074. 121 pp. MF–01; PC–05.

Bess, J.L. 1988. *Collegiality and Bureaucracy in the Modern University.* New York: Teachers College Press.

Biglan, A. 1973a. "The Characteristics of Subject Matter in Different Academic Areas." *Journal of Applied Psychology* 57: 195–203.

———. 1973b. "Relationship between Subject Matter Characteristics and the Structure and Output of University Departments." *Journal of Applied Psychology* 57: 204–13.

Birnbaum, R. 1983. *Maintaining Diversity in Higher Education.* San Francisco: Jossey-Bass.

———. 1988. *How Colleges Work: The Cybernetics of Academic Organization and Leadership.* San Francisco: Jossey-Bass.

Block, P. 1987. *The Empowered Manager: Positive Political Skills at Work.* San Francisco: Jossey-Bass.

Blocker, C.E., L.W. Bender, and S.V. Martorana. 1975. *The Political Terrain of American Postsecondary Education.* Fort Lauderdale, Fla.: Nova Univ. Press.

Boice, R. 1990. *Professors as Writers.* Stillwater, Okla.: New Forums Press.

———. 1991a. "New Faculty as Teachers." *Journal of Higher Education* 62: 150–73.

———. 1991b. "Quick Starters." In *Improving the Future of Teaching Improvement,* edited by M. Theall. New Directions for Teaching and Learning. San Francisco: Jossey-Bass.

———. 1992. *The New Faculty Member: Supporting and Fostering Professional Development.* San Francisco: Jossey-Bass.

Boice, R., and P.E. Myers. 1986. "Stresses and Satisfactions of Chairing in Psychology." *Professional Psychology: Research and Practice* 17: 200–204.

Bolman, J.G., and T.E. Deal. 1991. *Reframing Organizations: Artistry, Choice, and Leadership.* San Francisco: Jossey-Bass.

Booth, D.B. 1982. *The Department Chair: Professional Development and Role Conflict.* AAHE-ERIC Higher Education Research Report No. 10. Washington D.C.: American Association for Higher Education. ED 226 689. 60 pp. MF–01; PC–03.

Bowen, H., and J. Schuster. 1986. *American Professors: A National Resource Imperiled.* New York: Oxford Univ. Press.

Boyer, E.L. 1990. *Scholarship Reconsidered: Priorities of the Professoriate*. Princeton, N.J.: Carnegie Foundation for the Advancement of Teaching. ED 326 149. 151 pp. MF–01; PC–07.

Bragg, A.K. 1981. "The Socialization of Academic Department Heads: Past Patterns and Future Possibilities." Paper presented at an annual meeting of the Association for the Study of Higher Education, Washington, D.C. ED 203 813. 19 pp. MF–01; PC–01.

Brann, J., and T.A. Emmet. 1972. *The Academic Department of Division Chairman: A Complex Role*. Detroit: Balamp.

Braskamp, L.A., D.C. Brandenburg, and J.C. Ory. 1984. *Evaluating Teaching Effectiveness: A Practical Guide*. Beverly Hills, Calif.: Sage.

Bregman, N.J., and M.R. Moffett. 1991. "Funding Reality within Higher Education: Can Universities Cope?" In *Managing Institutions of Higher Education into the 21st Century: Issues and Implications,* edited by R.R. Sims and S.J. Sims. New York: Greenwood Press.

Brookes, J. 1988. "The Counseling Role of a Head of Department." Blagdon, Eng.: Further Education Staff College. ED 299 513. 9 p. MF–01; PC–01.

Brown, D.G., R.A. Scott, and L.C. Winner. 1987. "Academic and Administrative Officers." In *Key Resources on Higher Education Governance Management and Leadership,* edited by M.W. Peterson and L.A. Mets. San Francisco: Jossey-Bass.

Brown, J.D. 1977. "Departmental and University Leadership." In *Academic Departments,* edited by D.E. McHenry and Associates. San Francisco: Jossey-Bass.

Burgan, M. 1986. "Raiding, Targeting, and Meeting Outside Offers: Notes from Halfway through a Term." In *Profession 86*. New York: Modern Language Association of America.

Burns, J.M. 1978. *Leadership*. New York: Harper & Row.

Cahn, S.M., ed. 1990. *Morality, Responsibility, and the University: Studies in Academic Ethics*. Philadelphia: Temple Univ. Press.

Cameron, K.S., and M. Tschirhart. 1992. "Postindustrial Environments and Organizational Effectiveness in Colleges and Universities." *Journal of Higher Education* 63(1): 87–107.

Cameron, K.S., and D.O. Ulrich. 1986. "Transformational Leadership in Colleges and Universities." In *Higher Education: Handbook of Theory and Research,* edited by J.C. Smart. Vol. 2. New York: Agathon Press.

Caplow, T., and R.J. McGee. 1965. *The Academic Marketplace*. Garden City, N.Y.: Anchor Books.

Carnegie Foundation for the Advancement of Teaching. 1987. *A Classification of Institutions of Higher Education*. Princeton, N.J.: Author.

Carroll, J. 1990. "Career Paths of Department Chairs: A National Perspective." *Research in Higher Education* 32(6): 669–88.

Cashin, W.E. 1989. "Defining and Evaluating College Teaching."

IDEA Paper No. 21. Manhattan: Kansas State Univ., Center for Faculty Evaluation and Development. ED 339 731. 6 pp. MF–01; PC–01.

———. 1990. "Assessing Teaching Effectiveness." In *How Administrators Can Improve Teaching*, edited by P. Seldin and Associates. San Francisco: Jossey-Bass.

Chaffee, E.E., and W.G. Tierney. 1988. *Collegiate Culture and Leadership Strategies*. New York: ACE/Macmillan.

Clark, M.B., and F.H. Freeman, eds. 1990. *Leadership Education 1990: A Sourcebook*. Greensboro, N.C., and West Orange, N.J.: Center for Creative Leadership and Leadership Library of America.

Clinic to Improve University Teaching. 1974. "Teaching Analysis by Students (TABS)." Amherst: Univ. of Massachusetts–Amherst, School of Education.

Cobb, A.T. 1986. "Coalition Identification in Organizational Research." In *Research on Negotiation in Organizations*, edited by R.J. Leivici, B.H. Sheppard, and M.H. Bozerman. Vol. 1. London: JAI Press.

Cohen, M.D., and J.G. March. 1986. *Leadership and Ambiguity: The American College President*. 2d ed. Boston: Harvard Business School Press.

Collins, R. 1975. *Conflict Sociology*. New York: Academic Press.

———. 1979. *The Credential Society*. New York: Academic Press.

Corson, J.J. 1975. *The Governance of Colleges and Universities*. 2d ed. New York: McGraw-Hill.

Creswell, J.W. 1985. *Faculty Research Performance: Lessons from the Sciences and Social Sciences*. ASHE-ERIC Higher Education Report No. 4. Washington, D.C.: Association for the Study of Higher Education. ED 267 677. 92 pp. MF–01; PC–04.

Creswell, J.W., and M.L. Brown. 1992. "How Chairpersons Enhance Faculty Research: A Grounded Theory Study." *Review of Higher Education* 16(1): 41–62.

Creswell, J.W., and R.W. Roskens. 1981. "The Biglan Studies of Differences among Academic Areas." *Review of Higher Education* 4: 1–16.

Creswell, J.W., A.T. Seagren, and T.C. Henry. 1980. "Professional Development Training Needs of Departmental Chairpersons: A Test of the Biglan Model." *Planning and Changing* 10: 224–37.

Creswell, J.W., D.W. Wheeler, A.T. Seagren, N.J. Egly, and K.D. Beyer. 1990. *The Academic Chairperson's Handbook*. Lincoln: Univ. of Nebraska Press.

Curtis, E.T. 1990. "A Study of Role and Function of Division Chairs in the Washington State Community College System." *Dissertation Abstracts International* 51: AAD91–12913.

Davies, J.L., and A.W. Morgan. 1982. "The Politics of Institutional Change." In *Agenda for Institutional Change*, edited by L. Wagner. Surrey: Society for Research into Higher Education.

Deming, W.E. 1982. *Quality, Productivity, and Competitive Position.*

Cambridge, Mass.: MIT Center for Advanced Engineering Study.

Dill, D.D., and P.K. Fullagar. 1987. "Leadership and Administrative Style." In *Key Resources on Higher Education Governance Management and Leadership: A Guide to the Literature,* edited by M.W. Peterson and L.A. Mets. San Francisco: Jossey-Bass.

Donnithorne, L. 1992. "Institutional Politics and Planning." *Planning for Higher Education* 20: 13–18.

Dozier-Hackman, J. 1985. "Power Centrality in the Allocation of Resources in Colleges and Universities." *Administrative Science Quarterly* 30: 61–77.

Dressel, P.L., C.F. Johnson, and P.M. Marcus. 1971. *The Confidence Crisis: An Analysis of University Departments.* San Francisco: Jossey-Bass.

Duke, D.L. 1986. "The Aesthetics of Leadership." *Educational Administration Quarterly* 22: 7–27.

Eble, K.E. 1990a. "Chairpersons and Faculty Development." In *Enhancing Departmental Leadership: The Roles of the Chairperson,* edited by J.B. Bennett and D.J. Figuli. New York: ACE/Macmillan.

———. 1990b. "Communicating Effectively." In *Enhancing Departmental Leadership: The Roles of the Chairperson,* edited by J.B. Bennett and D.J. Figuli. New York: ACE/Macmillan.

Edgerton, R., P. Hutchins, and K. Quinlan. 1991. *The Teaching Portfolio: Capturing the Scholarship in Teaching.* Washington, D.C.: American Association for Higher Education. HE 026 149. 123 pp. MF–01; PC–05.

Elman, S.E., and S.M. Smock. 1985. *Professional Service and Faculty Rewards.* Washington, D.C.: National Association of State Universities and Land-Grant Colleges.

Falender, A.J. 1983. "Providing Focus for Financial Management." In *Management Techniques for Small and Specialized Institutions,* edited by A.J. Falender and J.C. Merson. New Directions for Higher Education No. 42. San Francisco: Jossey-Bass.

Falk, G. 1979. "The Academic Department Chairmanship and Role Conflict." *Improving College and University Teaching* 27(2): 79–86.

Fife, J. 1982. "Foreword." In *The Department Chair: Professional Development and Role Conflict,* by D.B. Booth. AAHE-ERIC Higher Education Research Report No. 10. Washington, D.C.: American Association for Higher Education. ED 226 689. 60 pp. MF–01; PC–03.

Fink, L.D. 1984. *The First Year of College Teaching.* New Directions for Teaching and Learning No. 17. San Francisco: Jossey-Bass.

Fisher, C.F. 1987. "Leadership Selection, Evaluation, and Development." In *Key Resources on Higher Education Governance Management and Leadership: A Guide to the Literature,* edited by M.W. Peterson and L.A. Mets. San Francisco: Jossey-Bass.

Fisher, R., and W. Ury. 1981. *Getting to Yes.* Boston: Houghton Mifflin.

Gardner, J.W. 1990. *Leadership.* New York: Free Press/Macmillan.

Gessner, Q. 1988. "The Politics of Continuing Higher Education." *Continuing Higher Education Review* 52(2): 67–77.

Glasser, J.P., and J.W. Tamm. 1991. "Better Bargaining." *Executive Educator* 5(3): 22–25.

Gmelch, W. 1989. "Intervention Strategies to Increase Faculty Productivity." Paper presented to the UCEA convention, Scottsdale, Arizona. Pullman, Wash.: Center for the Study of the Department Chair.

————. 1991. "The Stresses of Chairing a Department." *Department Chair* 1(3): 1.

Gmelch, W., and J.S. Burns. 1991. "Sources of Stress for Academic Department Chairs: A National Perspective." Paper presented at a meeting of the American Educational Research Association, Chicago, Illinois. ED 339 306. 31 pp. MF–01; PC–02.

Goffman, E. 1959. *The Presentation of Self in Everyday Life.* Garden City, N.Y.: Doubleday.

Goldberg, M. 1990. "Common and Uncommon Concerns: The Complex Role of the Community College Department Chair." In *Enhancing Departmental Leadership: The Roles of the Chairperson,* edited by J.B. Bennett and D.J. Figuli. New York: ACE/Macmillan.

Green, M., ed. 1989. *Minorities on Campus: A Handbook for Enhancing Diversity.* Washington, D.C.: American Council on Education.

Green, M., and S. McDade. 1991. *Investing in Higher Education: A Handbook of Leadership Development.* New York: ACE/Macmillan.

Groner, N.E. 1978. "Leadership Situations in Academic Departments: Relations among Measures of Situational Favorableness and Control." *Research in Higher Education* 8: 125–45.

Halpin, A.W. 1966. *Theory and Research in Administration.* New York: Macmillan.

Hardy, C., A. Langley, H. Mintzberg, and J. Rose. 1984. "Strategy Formulation in the University Setting." In *College and University Organization: Insights from Behavioral Sciences,* edited by J.L. Bess. New York: New York Univ.

Hearn, J.C., and R.B. Heydinger. 1985. "Scanning the External Environment of a University: Objectives, Constraints, and Possibilities." *Journal of Higher Education* 56(4): 419–45.

Heimler, C.H. 1972. "The College Departmental Chairman." In *The Academic Department or Division Chairman: A Complex Role,* edited by J. Brann and T.A. Emmet. Detroit: Balamp.

Henry, D.D. 1974. "The Academic Department and Educational Change." *Management Forum* 3(3): 1–4.

Heyns, R.W., ed. 1977. *Leadership for Higher Education: The Campus View.* Washington D.C.: American Council on Education.

Hitt, W.D. 1990. *Ethics in Leadership: Putting Theory into Practice.* Columbus, Ohio: Batelle Press.

Hynes, W.J. 1990. "Successful Proactive Recruiting Strategies: Quest for the Best." In *Enhancing Departmental Leadership: The Roles of the Chairperson,* edited by J.B. Bennett and D.J. Figuli. New York: ACE/Macmillan.

Jacobs, R. April 1986. "Types of Chairs." *Academic Leader.*

Jarvis, D.K. 1991. *Junior Faculty Development: A Handbook.* New York: Modern Language Association.

Jeffrey, R.C. 1985. "A Dean Interprets the Roles and Powers of an Ideal Chair." *Association for Communication Administration Bulletin* 52: 15–16.

Jennerich, E.J. 1981. "Competencies for Department Chairpersons: Myths and Realities." *Liberal Education* 67(1): 46–65.

Kanter, R. 1981. "Quality of Work Life and Work Behavior in Academia." *National Forum* 60: 35–38.

———. 1983. *The Change Masters: Innovations for Productivity in the American Corporation.* New York: Simon & Schuster.

Kerr, C. 1984. *Presidents Make a Difference: Strengthening Leadership in Colleges and Universities.* Washington, D.C.: Association of Governing Boards of Universities and Colleges. ED 247 879. 140 pp. MF–01; PC not available EDRS.

Kimble, G.A. 1974. "Background Materials for Chairman's Workshop." 5th ed. Materials prepared for a workshop given by the National Council of Graduate Departments of Psychology, American Psychological Association. ED 224 355. 90 pp. MF–01; PC–04.

———. 1979. *A Departmental Chairperson's Survival Manual.* New York: John Wiley & Sons.

Knight, W.H., and M.C. Holen. 1985. "Leadership and the Perceived Effectiveness of Department Chairpersons." *Journal of Higher Education* 56: 677–89.

Kniveton, B. 1989. *The Psychology of Bargaining.* Aldershol, U.K.: Avebury.

Kotter, J.P. 1988. *The Leadership Factor.* New York: Free Press.

Kouzes, J.M., and B.Z. Posner. 1987. *The Leadership Challenge: How to Get Extraordinary Things Done in Organizations.* San Francisco: Jossey-Bass.

Kremer-Hayon, L., and T.E. Avi-Izhak. 1986. "Roles of Academic Department Chairpersons at the University Level." *Journal of Higher Education* 15(1–2): 105–12.

Kroger-Hill, S.E., M.H. Bahniuk, and J. Dobos. 1989. "The Impact of Mentoring and Collegial Support on Faculty Success: An Analysis of Support Behavior, Information Adequacy, and Communication Apprehension." *Communication Education* 38:15–33.

Kuh, G.D., and E.J. Whitt. 1988. *The Invisible Tapestry: Culture in American Colleges and Universities.* ASHE-ERIC Higher Education Report No. 1. Washington D.C.: Association for the Study of Higher Education. ED 299 934. 160 pp. MF–01; PC–07.

Layzell, D.T., and J.W. Lyddon. 1990. *Budgeting for Higher Education at the State Level: Enigma, Paradox, and Ritual.* ASHE-ERIC Higher

Education Report No. 4. Washington, D.C.: George Washington Univ., School of Education and Human Development. ED 327 130. 134 pp. MF–01; PC–06.

Leary, M.R. 1988. "Self-Presentational Processes in Leadership Emergence and Effectiveness." In *Impression Management in the Organization,* edited by R.G. Giacalone and P. Rosenfeld. Hillsdale, N.J.: Erlbaum.

Lee, R., and P. Lawrence. 1985. *Organizational Behavior: Politics at Work.* London: Hutchinson.

Licata, C.M. 1986. *Post-tenure Faculty Evaluation: Threat or Opportunity?* ASHE-ERIC Higher Education Report No. 1. Washington, D.C.: Association for the Study of Higher Education. ED 270 009. 118 pp. MF–01; PC–05.

Lonsdale, A.J., and W.N. Bardsley. 1984. "Heads of Academic Departments: Responsibilities and Professional Development Needs." *Journal of Tertiary Educational Administration* 6(2): 117–27.

Lucas, A. 1989. *The Department Chairperson's Role in Enhancing College Teaching.* New Directions for Higher Education. San Francisco: Jossey-Bass.

———. 1990. "The Department Chair as Change Agent." In *How Administrators Can Improve Teaching,* edited by P. Seldin and Associates. San Francisco: Jossey-Bass.

Lunde, J.P., and T. Hartung. 1990. "Integrating Individual and Organizational Needs." In *Enhancing Faculty Careers: Strategies for Development and Renewal,* edited by J.H. Schuster and D.W. Wheeler. San Francisco: Jossey-Bass.

Lunde, J.P., D.W. Wheeler, T. Hartung, and B.J. Wheeler. 1991. "Second Order Change: Impact of a College Renewal Program over Time." *Innovative Higher Education* 16(2): 125–38.

Luthans, F. 1992. *Organizational Behavior.* 6th ed. New York: McGraw-Hill.

Luthans, F., R.M. Hodgetts, and S.A. Rosenkrantz. 1988. *Real Managers.* Cambridge, Mass.: Ballinger.

McCorkle, C.O., and S.O. Archibald. 1982. *Management and Leadership in Higher Education: Applying Modern Techniques of Planning, Resource Management, and Evaluation.* San Francisco: Jossey-Bass.

McDade, S.A. 1987. *Higher Education Leadership: Enhancing Skills through Professional Development Programs.* ASHE-ERIC Higher Education Report No. 5. Washington, D.C.: Association for the Study of Higher Education. ED 293 479. 138 pp. MF–01; PC–06.

McHenry, D.E., and Associates. 1977. *Academic Departments.* San Francisco: Jossey-Bass.

McKeachie, W.J. 1976. "Reactions from a Former Department Chairman." In *Examining Departmental Management,* edited by J.C. Smart and J.R. Montgomery. New Directions for Institutional Research No. 2. San Francisco: Jossey-Bass.

———. 1986. *Teaching Tips: A Guidebook for Beginning Teachers.* Lexington, Mass.: Heath.

McLaughlin, G.W., J.R. Montgomery, and L.F. Malpass. 1975. "Selected Characteristics, Roles, Goals, and Satisfactions of Department Chairmen in State and Land-grant Institutions." *Research in Higher Education* 3: 243–59.

Madison, D.L., R.W. Allen, L.W. Porter, P.A. Renwick, and B.T. Mayes. 1980. "Organizational Politics: An Exploration of Managers' Perceptions." *Human Relations* 33: 79–100.

Magana, A.E., and B.W. Neibel. 1980. "How Do Academic Administrators Spend—and Think They Spend—Their Time?" In *Insights into Engineering Education Administration,* edited by ASEE Publications Committee. Washington, D.C.: American Society for Engineering Education.

Mahoney, J. 1972. "Chairman as Messmaker." In *The Academic Department or Division Chairman: A Complex Role,* edited by J. Brann and T.A. Emmet. Detroit: Balamp.

Martorana, S.V., and E. Kuhns, eds. 1975. *Managing Academic Change: Interactive Forces and Leadership in Higher Education.* San Francisco: Jossey-Bass.

Maxcy, S.J. 1991. *Educational Leadership: A Critical Pragmatic Perspective.* New York: Bergin & Garvey.

May, W.T., ed. 1990. *Ethics in Higher Education.* New York: ACE/ Macmillan.

Menges, R., and C. Mathis. 1988. *Key Resources on Teaching, Learning, Curriculum, and Faculty Development: A Guide to the Higher Education Literature.* San Francisco: Jossey-Bass.

Miller, B.W., R.W. Hotes, and J.D. Terry. 1983. *Leadership in Higher Education: A Handbook for Practicing Administrators.* Westport, Conn.: Greenwood Press.

Miller, R. 1979. *The Assessment of College Performance: A Handbook of Techniques and Measures for Institutional Self-Evaluation.* San Francisco: Jossey-Bass.

———. 1987. *Evaluating Faculty for Promotion and Tenure.* San Francisco: Jossey-Bass.

Millichap, J. Winter 1986. "Contemporary Management Theory and the English Department." *ADE Bulletin* 85: 50–53.

Millis, B.J. 1991. "Putting the Teaching Portfolio in Context." In *To Improve the Academy,* edited by K.J. Zakorski. Stillwater, Okla.: New Forums Press.

Milne, F.L. 1988. "A House Undivided: Some Perspectives from a Once 'Intimate Enemy,' Now a Department Head." Paper presented at an annual meeting of the Conference on College Composition and Communication, St. Louis, Missouri. ED 294 234. 14 pp. MF–01; PC–01.

Minter, J. 1990. "Positioning the Department for Survival and Growth: An Exercise." In *Enhancing Departmental Leadership: The Roles of the Chairperson,* edited by J.B. Bennett and D.J. Figuli. New York: ACE/Macmillan.

Mintzberg, H. 1979. "Organizational Power and Goals: A Skeletal Theory." In *Strategic Management: A New View of Business Policy and Planning,* edited by D.E. Schendel and C.W. Hofer. Boston: Little, Brown.

Mitchell, M. 1987. "The Process of Department Leadership." *Review of Higher Education* 11(2): 161–76.

Monson, C.H. 1972. "The University of Utah's Department Chairmen Training Program." In *The Academic Department or Division Chairman: A Complex Role,* edited by J. Brann and T.A. Emmet. Detroit: Balamp.

Moomaw, W.E. 1984. "Participatory Leadership Strategy." In *Leadership Roles of Chief Academic Officers,* edited by D.G. Brown. New Directions for Higher Education No. 47. San Francisco: Jossey-Bass.

Moses, I. 1984. "The Role of the Head of Department in the Pursuit of Excellence." Paper presented at the Sixth International Conference on Higher Education, Univ. of Lancaster.

Moses, I., and E. Roe. 1990. *Heads and Chairs: Managing Academic Departments.* St. Lucia, Queensland, Australia: Univ. of Queensland Press.

Moxley, J.M., and G.A. Olson. 1988. "The Role of the Modern English Department Chair." Paper presented at an annual meeting of the Conference on College Composition and Communication, St. Louis, Missouri. ED 297 346. 22 pp. MF–01; PC–01.

Murray, R.K. 1964. "On Departmental Development: A Theory." *Journal of General Education* 6: 228–37.

Neumann, Y., and S.B. Boris. 1978. "Paradigm Development and Leadership Style of University Department Chairpersons." *Research in Higher Education* 9: 291–302.

Norton, S. 1980. "Academic Department Chair: Tasks and Responsibilities." Tempe: Arizona State Univ., Dept. of Educational Administration and Supervision.

Pappas, E.J. 1989. "The Department Chair in the 1990s: Confessions, Concerns, and Convictions." *ACA Bulletin* 68: 34–39.

Pascale, R.T. 1990. *Managing on the Edge.* New York: Simon & Schuster.

Patton, R.D. 1961. "Editorial: The Department Chairman." *Journal of Higher Education* 32: 459–61.

Peltason, J.W. 1984. "Foreword." In *Chairing the Academic Department: Leadership among Peers,* edited by A. Tucker. 2d ed. New York: ACE/Macmillan.

Pfeffer, J. 1981. *Power in Organizations.* Marshfield, Mass.: Pitman Press.

Pfeffer, J., G.R. Salanick, and H. Leblebici. 1976. "The Effect of Uncertainty on the Use of Social Influence in Organizational Decision

Making." *Administrative Science Quarterly* 21: 265–77.

Roach, J.H.L. 1976. "The Academic Department Chairperson: Roles and Responsibilities." *Educational Record* 57(1): 13–23.

"Roles of Department Chairs." 1992. *CSDC Newsletter* 2(3).

Rosovsky, H. 1990. *The University: An Owner's Manual.* New York: Norton.

Scanlon, W.F. 1986. *Alcoholism and Drug Abuse in the Workplace: Employee Assistance Programs.* New York: Praeger.

Schlenker, B.R. 1980. *Impression Management: The Self-Concept, Social Identity, and Interpersonal Relations.* Belmont, Calif.: Brooke/Cole.

Schnell, J. 1987. "Academic Chairpersons and the Management of Academic Departments in China." ED 291 294. 9 pp. MF–01; PC–01.

Schon, D. 1983. *The Reflective Practitioner: How Professionals Think in Action.* New York: Basic Books.

Schuster, J.H., D.W. Wheeler, and Associates. 1990. *Enhancing Faculty Careers.* San Francisco: Jossey-Bass.

Scott, R.A. 1981. "Portrait of a Departmental Chairperson." *AAHE Bulletin* 33: 1–6.

Seagren, A.T. 1978. "Perceptions of Administrative Tasks and Professional Development Needs by Chairpersons of Academic Departments: A Questionnaire." Lincoln: Univ. of Nebraska–Lincoln, Office of the Assistant Vice Chancellor for Program Development and Review, Task Force on Management Practices in Higher Education.

Seagren, A.T., and J.W. Creswell. 1985. "A Comparison of Perceptions of Administrative Tasks and Professional Development Needs of Chairpersons/Heads of Departments in Australia and the U.S." Paper presented at the Pan-Pacific Conference, Seoul, Korea. ED 275 328. 42 pp. MF–01; PC–02.

Seagren, A.T., and G. Filan. 1992. *The International Community College Chair Survey.* Mesa, Ariz., and Lincoln, Neb.: National Community College Chair Academy, Maricopa Community College, and Center for the Study of Higher and Postsecondary Education, Univ. of Nebraska–Lincoln.

Seagren, A.T., D.W. Wheeler, M. Mitchell, and J.W. Creswell. 1986. "Perception of Chairpersons and Faculty Concerning Roles, Descriptors, and Activities Important for Faculty Development and Departmental Vitality." Unpublished manuscript. Lincoln: Univ. of Nebraska–Lincoln, Dept. of Educational Administration. ED 276 387. 33 pp. MF–01; PC–02.

Seedorf, R.G., and W.H. Gmelch. 1989. "The Department Chair: A Descriptive Study." Paper presented at an annual meeting of the American Educational Research Association, San Francisco, California. ED 309 713. 21 pp. MF–01; PC–01.

Seldin, P. 1980. *Successful Faculty Evaluation Programs.* Crugers,

N.Y.: Coventry.

———. 1984. *Changing Practices in Faculty Evaluation.* San Francisco: Jossey-Bass.

———. 1991. *The Teaching Portfolio: A Practical Guide to Improved Performance and Promotion/Tenure Decisions.* Bolton, Mass.: Anker.

———. 1992. "Recognizing and Rewarding Good Teaching." Presentation at the National Education Association Conference on Higher Education, San Diego, California.

Seldin, P., and Associates, eds. 1990. *How Administrators Can Improve Teaching.* San Francisco: Jossey-Bass.

Seldin, P., P. Hutchins, and B. Millis. 1992. "The Teaching Portfolio and Its Purposes: A Look at Current Practice." Paper presented at a meeting of the American Association for Higher Education, Chicago, Illinois.

Senge, P. 1991. *The Fifth Discipline: The Art and Practice of the Learning Organization.* New York: Doubleday.

Sherr, L.A., and D.J. Teeter, eds. 1991. *Total Quality Management in Education.* New Directions for Institutional Research No. 71. San Francisco: Jossey-Bass.

Shreeve, W., B.W. Brucker, and J.J. Martin. 1987. "University Department Chairs: Who Are We?" Unpublished manuscript. Cheney, Wash.: Eastern Washington Univ., Dept. of Education. ED 285 464. 17 pp. MF–01; PC–01.

Shulman, L. 1989. "Toward a Pedagogy of Substance." *AAHE Bulletin.* Washington, D.C.: American Association for Higher Education.

Smart, J.C., and C.F. Elton. 1976. "Administrative Roles of Department Chairmen." In *Examining Departmental Management,* edited by J.C. Smart and J.R. Montgomery. New Directions for Institutional Research No. 2. San Francisco: Jossey-Bass.

Sorcinelli, M.D., and A. Austin, eds. 1992. *Developing New and Junior Faculty.* New Directions for Teaching and Learning. San Francisco: Jossey-Bass.

Startup, R. 1976. "The Role of the Department Head." *Studies in Higher Education* 1(2): 233–43.

Summers, S.R. 1991. "Financing the American Community College in the 1990s: A New Kind of Blues or the Same Old Tune?" Gainesville: Univ. of Florida, Interinstitutional Research Council. ED 336 146. 27 pp. MF–01; PC–02.

Tedeschi, J.T., and V. Melburg. 1984. "Impression Management and Influence in Organizations." *Research in the Sociology of Organizations* 3: 31–58.

Thoreson, R.W., and E.P. Hosakawa. 1984. *Employee Assistance Programs in Higher Education.* Springfield, Ill.: Charles C. Thomas.

Tierney, W.G. 1988. "Organizational Culture in Higher Education." *Journal of Higher Education* 59(1): 2–21.

Trow, M. 1977. "Departments as Contexts for Teaching and Learning."

In *Academic Departments,* edited by D.E. McHenry and Associates. San Francisco: Jossey-Bass.

Tucker, A. 1984. *Chairing the Academic Department: Leadership among Peers.* 2d ed. New York: ACE/Macmillan.

———. 1992. *Chairing the Academic Department: Leadership among Peers.* 3d ed. New York: ACE/Macmillan.

Tucker, A., and R.A. Bryan. 1988. *The Academic Dean: Dove, Dragon, and Diplomat.* New York: ACE/Macmillan.

Underwood, D. 1972. "The Chairman as Academic Planner." In *The Academic Department or Division Chairman: A Complex Role,* edited by J. Brann and T.A. Emmet. Detroit: Balamp.

Urbach, F. 1992. *Seven Dimensions for Documenting Teaching.* IUSB Faculty Development Monograph. South Bend: Indiana Univ. at South Bend, Faculty Development Office.

Vroom, V.H. 1983. "Leaders and Leadership in Academe." *Review of Higher Education* 6: 367–86.

Waerdt, L.V. 1990. "Women in Academic Departments: Uneasy Roles, Complex Relationships." In *Enhancing Departmental Leadership: The Roles of the Chairperson,* edited by J.B. Bennett and D.J. Figuli. New York: ACE/Macmillan.

Waltzer, H. 1975. *The Job of Academic Department Chairman.* Washington, D.C.: American Council on Education.

Warren, C.O. 1990. "Chairperson and Dean: The Essential Partnership." In *Enhancing Departmental Leadership,* edited by J.B. Bennett and D.J. Figuli. New York: ACE/Macmillan.

Watson, R.E.L. 1986. "The Role of the Department Chair: A Replication and Extension." *Canadian Journal of Higher Education* 16(1): 13–23.

Weber, M. 1947. *The Theory of Social and Economic Organization.* New York: Oxford Univ. Press.

Weick, K. 1978. "Educational Organizations as Loosely Coupled Systems." *Administrative Science Quarterly* 23: 541–52.

Weimer, M., M. Kerns, and J. Parrett. 1988. "Instructional Observations: Caveats, Concerns, and Ways to Compensate." *Studies in Higher Education* 13(3): 299–307.

Weinberg, S.S. 1984. "The Perceived Responsibilities of the Departmental Chairperson: A Note of a Preliminary Study." *Higher Education* 13: 301–3.

Welsh, M.A., and E.A. Slusher. 1986. "Organizational Design as a Context for Political Activity." *Administrative Science Quarterly* 31: 389–402.

Wendel, F.C., and W. Sybouts. 1988. "Assessment Center Methods in Educational Administration." UCEA Monograph Series. Tempe, Ariz.: Univ. Council on Educational Administration.

Wheeler, D.W. 1990. "Faculty Career Consulting." In *Enhancing Faculty Careers: Strategies for Development and Renewal,* edited by J.H. Schuster and D.W. Wheeler. San Francisco: Jossey-Bass.

Whitmore, J. 1988. *Handbook for Theater Department Chairs.* Annandale, Va.: Association for Communications Administration. ED 305 855. 110 pp. MF–01; PC–05.

Wolverton, R.E. 1990. "Chairing the Small Department." In *Enhancing Departmental Leadership: The Roles of the Chairperson,* edited by J.B. Bennett and D.J. Figuli. New York: ACE/Macmillan.

Yuker, H.E. 1984. *Faculty Workload: Research, Theory, and Interpretation.* ASHE-ERIC Higher Education Report No. 10. Washington, D.C.: Association for the Study of Higher Education. ED 259 691. 120 pp. MF–01; PC–05.

Yukl, G.A. 1989. *Leadership in Organizations.* 2d ed. Englewood Cliffs, N.J.: Prentice-Hall.

INDEX

E

effectiveness. See recommendations to improve chair effectiveness
ethics, 77
evaluation of chair. See performance evaluation of chair
    exemplification, 40

F

faculty
        autonomy and authority, 12, 21
        development, 51–57, 75, 77
        evaluation, 45–52, 77
        peer ratings, 48–49
        performance indicators, 50–51
        personal concerns, 57
        recruitment and retention, 77
        remotivation, 56–57
        research and publication, 55–56
        student ratings, 47–48
        teaching, 48–49, 54–55
        workload, 77
federal policy, 36–37
Ford Motor Company, 26
formative evaluation, 52
Fund for the Improvement of Post Secondary Education, 55
funding, 76

G

gender. See diversity and gender

H

human resource frame, 74

I

IDEA (Instructional Development and Effectiveness Assessment),
    52
impression management, 39–41
influence, 31–33
information, use of, 3, 25, 32–33, 38, 43, 63, 78, 80
ingratiation, 40
Institute of Agriculture and Natural Resources. See University
    of Nebraska-Lincoln
institutional development, 76
institutional types, influence on chair, 59–66
interest groups and coalitions, 33–34
International Institute for Academic Leadership
    Development, 69, 78
intimidation, 40

K

Kansas State Chair Conference, 78
Kansas State University, 65, 78
Kellogg Foundation,69

L

leadership, 17–26
    frames, 74–76
    goals, 24–25
    personal characteristics, 32
    research on, 20–22
    skills, 22–26, 39, 62–63, 78–79
    strategies, 37–43
    theories of, 17–21
    transformations, 19–20, 25, 74
    transition, 80–81
    vision, 19–20, 25–26, 81
Leadership Behavior Description Questionnaire (LBDQ), 65
learned helplessness, xv-xvi
loosely coupled systems, 29, 60–61

M

Maricopa Community College, 8, 69
mentoring, 53–54, 78, 80–81
minority participation, 77
Modern Language Association of America, 69

N

National Academy for Community College Chairs, 8, 69
National Association of Secondary School Principals
    Assessment Center Project, 8
National Community College Chair Conference, 78
Nebraska Project, 8
negative feedback loops, 61
negotiation and bargaining, 42–43
networking and support gathering, 41

O

office power, 31–32
Ohio State University, 65
open systems, 34
organizational
    culture, 60
    decision making theories, 29–30
    environment and leadership, 18–19, 26, 41
    politics, 30–31
organized anarchy model, 29–30, 60

P

performance evaluation of chair, 64–65
persuasion strategies, 38
Pfeffer's definition of organizational politics, 31
political
     environments, 31, 34–37
     frame, 75
     model, 29–30, 60
     strategies, 37–43
     portfolios. See teaching portfolios
     power sources, 30–34, 63
preparatory strategies, 39
preventative strategies, 38
principled bargaining, 42
professional development and training of chairs, xvi, 7, 11, 24–26,
    65–70, 78–80, 89
promotion and tenure, 52
pull strategies, 38
push strategies, 37

Q

quality control, 76

R

rational skills, 62–63
recommendations to improve chair effectiveness, 81–83
reflective practice, 79
roles and responsibilities of chair. See also faculty;
leadership
     administrative views, 10, 12–13
     ambiguity and conflict, xv–xvi, 10–14, 22, 69, 73
     checklist, 73–74, 85–87
     faculty views, 9–10, 12–13
     importance of chair role, 1–4
     major tasks, 5–10, 64–65
     research on, 5–10
     stress, 14–15
     workload, 14

S

"scholarship reconsidered" concept, 51
state legislation, 36
State University of Florida system, 69
strategies. See political strategies
structural frame, 75
summative evaluation, 51–52
swivel effect, 1

symbolic
    acts, 61
    frame, 75

T

TABS (Teaching Analysis by Students), 52
teaching portfolios, 48–49
Total Quality Management, 26, 76
training of chairs. See professional development and training
   of chairs

U

University of California system, 22
University of Nebraska-Lincoln
    Center for the Study of Higher and Postsecondary
      Education, 8, 69
    Institute of Agriculture and Natural Resources, 56
unobtrusive management, 61

W

Weber, Max, 60
win-win method, 42

ASHE-ERIC HIGHER EDUCATION REPORTS

Since 1983, the Association for the Study of Higher Education (ASHE) and the Educational Resources Information Center (ERIC) Clearinghouse on Higher Education, a sponsored project of the School of Education and Human Development at The George Washington University, have cosponsored the *ASHE-ERIC Higher Education Report* series. The 1993 series is the twenty-second overall and the fifth to be published by the School of Education and Human Development at the George Washington University.

Each monograph is the definitive analysis of a tough higher education problem, based on thorough research of pertinent literature and institutional experiences. Topics are identified by a national survey. Noted practitioners and scholars are then commissioned to write the reports, with experts providing critical reviews of each manuscript before publication.

Eight monographs (10 before 1985) in the ASHE-ERIC Higher Education Report series are published each year and are available on individual and subscription bases. Subscription to eight issues is $98.00 annually; $78 to members of AAHE, AIR, or AERA; and $68 to ASHE members. All foreign subscribers must include an additional $10 per series year for postage.

To order, use the order form on the last page of this book. Regular prices are as follows:

Series	Price	Series	Price
1993	$18.00	1985 to 87	$10.00
1990 to 92	17.00	1983 and 84	7.50
1988 and 89	15.00	before 1983	6.50

Discounts on non-subscription orders:
- Bookstores, and current members of AERA, AIR, AAHE and ASHE, receive a 25% discount.
- Bulk: For non-bookstore, non-member orders of 10 or more books, deduct 10%.

Shipping costs are as follows:
- U.S. address: 5% of invoice subtotal for orders over $50.00; $2.50 for each order with an invoice subtotal of $50.00 or less.
- Foreign: $2.50 per book.

All orders under $45.00 must be prepaid. Make check payable to ASHE-ERIC. For Visa or MasterCard, include card number, expiration date and signature.

Address order to
ASHE-ERIC Higher Education Reports
The George Washington University
1 Dupont Circle, Suite 630
Washington, DC 20036
Or phone (202) 296-2597
Write or call for a complete catalog.

1992 ASHE-ERIC Higher Education Reports

1. The Leadership Compass: Values and Ethics in Higher Education
   John R. Wilcox and Susan L. Ebbs

2. Preparing for a Global Community: Achieving an International Perspective in Higher Education
   Sarah M. Pickert

3. Quality: Transforming Postsecondary Education
   Ellen Earle Chaffee and Lawrence A. Sherr

4. Faculty Job Satisfaction: Women and Minorities in Peril
   Martha Wingard Tack and Carol Logan Patitu

5. Reconciling Rights and Responsibilities of Colleges and Students: Offensive Speech, Assembly, Drug Testing, and Safety
   Annette Gibbs

6. Creating Distinctiveness: Lessons from Uncommon Colleges and Universities
   Barbara K. Townsend, L. Jackson Newell, and Michael D. Wiese

7. Instituting Enduring Innovations: Achieving Continuity of Change in Higher Education
   Barbara K. Curry

8. Crossing Pedagogical Oceans: International Teaching Assistants in U.S. Undergraduate Education
   Rosslyn M. Smith, Patricia Byrd, Gayle L. Nelson, Ralph Pat Barrett, and Janet C. Constantinides

1991 ASHE-ERIC Higher Education Reports

1. Active Learning: Creating Excitement in the Classroom
   Charles C. Bonwell and James A. Eison

2. Realizing Gender Equality in Higher Education: The Need to Integrate Work/Family Issues
   Nancy Hensel

3. Academic Advising for Student Success: A System of Shared Responsibility
   Susan H. Frost

4. Cooperative Learning: Increasing College Faculty Instructional Productivity
   David W. Johnson, Roger T. Johnson, and Karl A. Smith

5. High School–College Partnerships: Conceptual Models, Programs, and Issues
   Arthur Richard Greenberg

6. Meeting the Mandate: Renewing the College and Departmental Curriculum
   William Toombs and William Tierney

7. Faculty Collaboration: Enhancing the Quality of Scholarship
   and Teaching
   Ann E. Austin and Roger G. Baldwin

8. Strategies and Consequences: Managing the Costs in Higher
   Education
   John S. Waggaman

1990 ASHE-ERIC Higher Education Reports

1. The Campus Green: Fund Raising in Higher Education
   Barbara E. Brittingham and Thomas R. Pezzullo

2. The Emeritus Professor: Old Rank - New Meaning
   James E. Mauch, Jack W. Birch, and Jack Matthews

3. "High Risk" Students in Higher Education: Future Trends
   Dionne J. Jones and Betty Collier Watson

4. Budgeting for Higher Education at the State Level: Enigma,
   Paradox, and Ritual
   Daniel T. Layzell and Jan W. Lyddon

5. Proprietary Schools: Programs, Policies, and Prospects
   John B. Lee and Jamie P. Merisotis

6. College Choice: Understanding Student Enrollment Behavior
   Michael B. Paulsen

7. Pursuing Diversity: Recruiting College Minority Students
   Barbara Astone and Elsa Nuñez-Wormack

8. Social Consciousness and Career Awareness: Emerging Link
   in Higher Education
   John S. Swift, Jr.

1989 ASHE-ERIC Higher Education Reports

1. Making Sense of Administrative Leadership: The 'L' Word in
   Higher Education
   Estela M. Bensimon, Anna Neumann, and Robert Birnbaum

2. Affirmative Rhetoric, Negative Action: African-American and
   Hispanic Faculty at Predominantly White Universities
   Valora Washington and William Harvey

3. Postsecondary Developmental Programs: A Traditional Agenda
   with New Imperatives
   Louise M. Tomlinson

4. The Old College Try: Balancing Athletics and Academics in
   Higher Education
   John R. Thelin and Lawrence L. Wiseman

5. The Challenge of Diversity: Involvement or Alienation in the Academy?
   Daryl G. Smith

6. Student Goals for College and Courses: A Missing Link in Assessing and Improving Academic Achievement
   Joan S. Stark, Kathleen M. Shaw, and Malcolm A. Lowther

7. The Student as Commuter: Developing a Comprehensive Institutional Response
   Barbara Jacoby

8. Renewing Civic Capacity: Preparing College Students for Service and Citizenship
   Suzanne W. Morse

1988 ASHE-ERIC Higher Education Reports

1. The Invisible Tapestry: Culture in American Colleges and Universities
   George D. Kuh and Elizabeth J. Whitt

2. Critical Thinking: Theory, Research, Practice, and Possibilities
   Joanne Gainen Kurfiss

3. Developing Academic Programs: The Climate for Innovation
   Daniel T. Seymour

4. Peer Teaching: To Teach is To Learn Twice
   Neal A. Whitman

5. Higher Education and State Governments: Renewed Partnership, Cooperation, or Competition?
   Edward R. Hines

6. Entrepreneurship and Higher Education: Lessons for Colleges, Universities, and Industry
   James S. Fairweather

7. Planning for Microcomputers in Higher Education: Strategies for the Next Generation
   Reynolds Ferrante, John Hayman, Mary Susan Carlson, and Harry Phillips

8. The Challenge for Research in Higher Education: Harmonizing Excellence and Utility
   Alan W. Lindsay and Ruth T. Neumann

1987 ASHE-ERIC Higher Education Reports

1. Incentive Early Retirement Programs for Faculty: Innovative Responses to a Changing Environment
   Jay L. Chronister and Thomas R. Kepple, Jr.

2. Working Effectively with Trustees: Building Cooperative Campus Leadership
   Barbara E. Taylor

1985 ASHE-ERIC Higher Education Reports

1. Flexibility in Academic Staffing: Effective Policies and Practices
   Kenneth P. Mortimer, Marque Bagshaw, and Andrew T. Masland

2. Associations in Action: The Washington, D.C. Higher Education Community
   Harland G. Bloland

3. And on the Seventh Day: Faculty Consulting and Supplemental Income
   Carol M. Boyer and Darrell R. Lewis

4. Faculty Research Performance: Lessons from the Sciences and Social Sciences
   John W. Creswell

5. Academic Program Review: Institutional Approaches, Expectations, and Controversies
   Clifton F. Conrad and Richard F. Wilson

6. Students in Urban Settings: Achieving the Baccalaureate Degree
   Richard C. Richardson, Jr. and Louis W. Bender

7. Serving More Than Students: A Critical Need for College Student Personnel Services
   Peter H. Garland

8. Faculty Participation in Decision Making: Necessity or Luxury?
   Carol E. Floyd

---

*Out-of-print. Available through EDRS. Call 1-800-443-ERIC.